ENTERPRISE EXCELLENCE | SERIES

GREEN MANUFACTURING

D1040671

Series Mission

To share new ideas and examples of excellence through case studies and other reports from all types of organizations, and to show how both leading-edge and proven improvement methods can be applied to a range of operations and industries.

ENTERPRISE EXCELLENCE|SERIES

GREEN
MANUFACTURING

Case Studies in Lean and Sustainability

Association for Manufacturing Excellence
(AME)

3 1336 08076 1050

Most Productivity Press books are available at quantity discounts when purchased in bulk. For more information contact our Customer Service Department (888-319-5852). Address all other inquiries to:

Productivity Press
444 Park Avenue South, 7th Floor
New York, NY 10016
United States of America
Telephone: 212-686-5900
Fax: 212-686-5411
E-mail: info@productivitypress.com

ProductivityPress.com

Material originally appeared in *Target*.

Library of Congress Cataloging-in-Publication Data

Green manufacturing : case studies in lean and sustainability /
Association for Manufacturing Excellence (AME).
    p. cm. — (Enterprise excellence series)
    Includes index.
    ISBN 978-1-56327-389-6 (alk. paper)
1. Industrial management—Environmental aspects. 2. Production
management—Environmental aspects. 3. Manufacturing industries
—Environmental aspects. I. Association for Manufacturing
Excellence (U.S.)
    HD30.255.G742 2007
    658.5'1—dc22

                                                        2007037623

11   10   09   08   07   5   4   3   2   1

Contents

Foreword

In 2003, a member of Baxter's environment, health and safety (EHS) group presented at the Association for Manufacturing Excellence's (AME) annual conference. The presentation addressed the work Baxter International Inc. had been doing to integrate EHS principles into lean manufacturing initiatives. We welcomed the opportunity to be part of a conference that hadn't typically involved our environmental colleagues. That year, of the six tracks of presentations for the week, our presentation was the only one that addressed environmental improvement efforts in manufacturing. In contrast, the 2007 AME conference incorporated an entire track devoted to the environment: "Lean and Green," and featured Hunter Lovins, a well-known and respected sustainability advocate and researcher, as a conference keynote speaker.

Those of us who have worked in the EHS field for many years are witnessing a welcome change. Due perhaps to the rising cost of energy, raw materials and waste disposal, as well as increased attention on global warming, more and more companies are recognizing that environmental stewardship brings business value. Particularly in large multinationals, EHS professionals are seen as integral to a company's success. Using manufacturing tools like lean to address environmental issues and goals gives EHS further credibility and demonstratively adds business value.

Baxter has held environmental stewardship as a priority for more than two decades, and has been a pioneer in the areas of environmental financial reporting; management of EHS data; and establishing, tracking progress against and reporting on specific environmental goals — including greenhouse gas emissions. Baxter recognizes that the health of the planet affects the health of the people who inhabit it — we understand this connection and work to improve both.

Over the years, we have sustained our leadership and commitment to reducing our environmental footprint and have advanced the health and welfare of the communities in which we operate. A key driver for these initiatives at Baxter has been the realization that sound environmental practices can contribute to, and in some cases, drive competitive advantage.

The benefits transcend mere cost avoidance and energy or raw-material savings. Many of the initiatives we have put in place in our facilities also have brought higher production throughput, higher quality levels, greater production flexibility and optimization of manufacturing assets, as well as reduced scrap material and waste. Perhaps more importantly, we have achieved greater employee engagement by tapping into our employees' passion for the health of the planet and society and by applying it to improvements in our production processes and workplace safety.

But despite our long-term commitment and focus, in 2000, we found performance in reducing environmental waste and energy was lagging. Data showed that traditional pollution-prevention techniques, which generally involved "waste minimization teams" and focused on recycling, were no longer working. It was in that year that Baxter began to aggressively deploy lean techniques and, from the start, EHS professionals were involved. By integrating EHS expertise into our lean manufacturing initiatives, we were not only able to prevent negative environmental consequences, but also to identify new opportunities for improvement.

We continue today experimenting with various approaches to integrating EHS into lean. One approach is simply to apply environmental metrics, such as waste, water use, and emissions-generation rates, to such commonly used lean tools as value stream maps. We can add goals for improvements in these metrics to "future-state maps" that then become the focus of kaizen rapid-improvement events. Another approach is to apply lean tools to EHS-focused processes, such as wastewater treatment or safety-incident investigations, to make EHS processes more efficient. We have used traditional value stream mapping, for example, in areas such as nurse stations, to improve case management flow and move employees back onto the production floor faster. Yet another approach is to slightly modify traditional lean tools, such as value stream maps, to understand and "learn to see" flow of water, energy, raw materials, or other utility processes. The Baxter case study included in this collection illustrates how we apply this technique to reduce water use. A fourth approach is to integrate traditional pollution-prevention techniques, such as process mapping and resource accounting into lean and clean tools to provide a new way of systematically looking at waste-reduction opportunities. This enables plant personnel to see and think about their processes differently, which inspires innovative solutions. In addition, using these modified lean techniques helps EHS become much more integrated into everyday operations and the business.

World-class manufacturing requires excellence in design, process, purchasing, quality, and EHS. Successful, world-class companies tap all of these areas of expertise in a seamless manner to reduce waste, drive efficiency, and increase productivity. By trying different approaches and actively working for process improvement, our work to achieve world-class manufacturing has generated several success stories that help bring attention and support, both internally and externally. Our environmental performance, which has been included every year in our sustainability report since 2001, shows the success of these efforts.

Baxter is happy to have had the opportunity to work with other companies and with government to share our experiences and learn from each other. We see tremendous value in sharing ideas, practical advice, and best practices within our own organization and through such formal industry and agency collaborations as the U.S. Environmental Protection Agency's Lean Manufacturing (under the Office of Policy and Innovation), and Green Supplier Network programs. The EPA's "Lean and Environment Toolkit" and website at www.epa.gov/lean, as well as *Target* magazine and the AME organization, serve as valuable clearinghouses for sharing across companies and industries.

The significant challenge the world faces in developing a sustainable future requires the best minds working together, from all disciplines and backgrounds, to find and implement innovative, effective solutions. We consider the publication of this collection of *Target* articles and EPA case studies as an important step, and hope that others will continue to share and promote new approaches and ideas.

Jenni Cawein and Rob Currie
Environment, Health and Safety
Baxter International Inc.

Introduction

Growing numbers of businesses are coming to recognize that sustainability is an important concept. Adopting practices designed to protect the environment and minimize energy use is not only a good idea, but also good business, as it can reduce costs and prevent problems.

Companies are also realizing that lean principles can readily be used to support sustainable practices. First, a lean approach can reduce waste and save energy. In addition, lean methods can be applied to identify and measure environmental wastes so that opportunities for improvement become clear.

This book focuses on how businesses are using lean strategies to help them operate in ways that are environmentally responsible. The case studies and other information on these pages can provide you with ideas regarding what your company can do to help preserve and protect the environment in the most efficient, cost-effective manner possible.

The first two sections of this book feature articles originally published in *Target*, the magazine of the Association for Manufacturing Excellence. These in-depth articles contain the kind of detail and sharp insights well-known to the magazine's readers.

Section One, Protecting the Environment, begins with an essay by consultant Gary Langenwalter, who lays a foundation for the rest of the book. In Chapter One, he discusses the importance of sustainability, the benefits of sustainable strategies and ways in which a lean approach can help implement those strategies.

In Chapter Two, Mitch Kidwell of the Environmental Protection Agency extends that discussion. He explains that EPA is embracing the concept of pursuing environmental goals through lean initiatives and provides examples of companies that are reaping the benefits of this strategy. He also describes The Lean and Environment Toolkit developed by EPA.

Chapter Three is a case study of DuPont, which has focused on sustainability since 1989. Dawn Rittenhouse of DuPont explains the keys to success of the company's sustainable growth model, its goals, its research, its metrics and the ways it listens to customers, works with supply chain partners and shares knowledge internally to make that model a reality.

Reverse logistics — broadly defined to include recycling and reuse of a product and its packaging — is the focus of Chapter Four. Read here how government programs in several countries support this approach, and how Coors and Dell are involved in these types of recycling programs.

Section Two is devoted to articles on the wise use and conservation of energy.

Chapter Five describes the efforts of many different companies to achieve energy savings. This chapter also includes helpful suggestions on how your company can tackle energy issues, plus a list of energy management references and resources.

Chapters Six and Seven were originally published as a two-part series on The Future of Energy in Manufacturing. Written by consultant and energy professional Dr. John R. Wilson, these chapters review the sources and future availability of conventional fossil fuels, plus the advantages and disadvantages of alternative fuels, such as hydrogen, biodiesel, and other possible biofuels as well as the future role of coal as a source for synthetic natural gas.

The third section of this book consists of three case studies developed by EPA.

The company profiled in Chapter Eight is 3M. Chapter Five had mentioned 3M's efforts in energy conservation; this case study presents a broad but detailed description of the company's dedication to sustainability and its use of lean and six sigma initiatives in those efforts.

Baxter Healthcare is studied in Chapter Nine. The case study describes a water value stream mapping exercise held at one of the company's facilities and how that project resulted in plans to reduce water consumption and save money with little or no capital investment.

And Chapter Ten explains how a variety of lean initiatives at General Motors produced benefits ranging from a decrease in the use of paint-cleaning solvent to a reduction in waste during production of plastic parts to less use of paper in Request for Quote processes.

Operating in an environmentally responsible way has never been more important. This book can provide you with insights and ideas that will help you transform your operations to support sustainability.

Section I

Improving
Processess

1

"Life" is Our Ultimate Customer: From Lean to Sustainability

Gary Langenwalter

In Brief

Environmentally sustainable practices are a natural extension of lean operational philosophy and techniques. Sustainability can pay off in the short-term, not just the long term. Using examples, the article is an overview of both the why-to and some of the how-to of sustainability, with emphasis on how it follows from lean manufacturing.

For decades, Lean Manufacturing has been the best way to run a manufacturing company, and lean principles have been successfully applied in many other industries, including banking, hospitals, and government. However, we have two fundamental challenges:

1. In spite of our best efforts, the U.S. economy as a whole is massively inefficient. Only 6 percent of materials actually end up in products.[1] Total wastes in the United States, excluding wastewater, now exceed 50 trillion pounds per year.[2]

2. Short-term financial returns always trump longer-term issues such as caring for the environment and social well-being until the long term suddenly becomes short term — like Katrina. Then our short-sightedness becomes glaringly obvious. We must start becoming serious about our environment and society in order to sustain our companies, our nation, and our world. The irony and tragedy inherent in this situation is that most decision-makers assume that sustainability has a low financial return. In reality, sustainability can return its investment within 6-to-12 months,

1

enabling a company to justify the investment on a purely short-term economic standpoint.

Sustainability is "meeting the needs of the current generation without compromising the ability of future generations to meet their needs."[3] It's the Golden Rule applied across generations. Lean leads us toward sustainability initiatives. Lean tools apply to any kind of problem, including environmental ones. The lean mantra of eliminating waste fits sustainability initiatives perfectly. Because it is much like lean both in concept and practice, sustainability can be thought of as lean extended to a much broader objective.

Sustainability (like lean) has a good track record of improving company finances because of the emphasis on eliminating waste and the substantial increase in creativity by employees at all levels. For example, Timberland, which is trying to "use the resources, energy, and profits of a publicly traded footwear-and-apparel company to combat social ills, help the environment, and improve conditions for laborers around the world," has achieved the following financial results over the last five years:[4]

A study of companies over an 11-year period demonstrates that "stakeholder-balanced companies show four times the sales growth and eight times the employment growth of companies that focus solely on shareholders."[5]

Sustainability continues broadening a company's outlook, begun with lean. It is a four-way win:

- Owners: Profitability and stock values normally increase.
- Executives: Better financial performance enhances careers. Additionally, executives create a legacy of passing on real value to their grandchildren.
- Employees: People prefer to work with environmentally sustainable and socially supportive operations. Like lean, sustainability requires their commitment.
- Communities: They support companies that care about their long-term health and viability.

Financial Results of Timberland, An Environmentally Responsible Company

Sales	Up 9.7% per year
Earnings per share	Up 20% per year
Stock price	Up 64%

Figure 1.

Sustainability is important to all of us; therefore it applies to all sizes of organizations. As with lean, no operation is too small to engage in it and to benefit from it. As with lean, sustainability requires a change in outlook, thinking, and working culture. Lean focuses on the economic customer; in sustainability, life itself is our ultimate customer.

What is Sustainability?

The viewpoint of sustainability is the opposite of financial short-term thinking. Like lean, it stresses closed-loop, cyclical thinking rather than linear, goal-oriented thinking. It actually goes even farther, into whole-system thinking, which causes practitioners to look for long-term unintended consequences of their decisions.

Conventional business has assumed an inexhaustible supply of raw material from nature. It has used a "take-make-waste" model, in which virtually all materials eventually wind up in a landfill from which they cannot easily be used by future generations. For 200 years we have been able to find substitutes, often better ones, for materials that were running out, like petroleum for whale oil, or synthetic rubber for natural rubber during World War II. We will continue to improve materials, but this model is not sustainable for the long term, because every material that is easy to obtain will already be in use.

In contrast, sustainability assumes that resources are finite, and therefore that resources should be re-used, and re-used again, and again, so that they are kept in use "forever." Instead of linear, thinking becomes closed loop, or cradle-to-cradle it is sometimes called. Additionally, in sustainability thinking, anything that damages the ability of earth to sustain life should be reduced or eliminated. Viewed in this way, the take-make-waste model is both appallingly wasteful and highly detrimental.

Instead we can intentionally redesign our processes so that our outflows become useful inflows to other processes. In CFO terms, instead of us paying to have trash hauled away; customers should pay us for raw material that they can use. Like some lean practices, this sounds highly simplistic, and it is; it takes time to implement, and implementation uncovers one practical problem after another in need of solution. But like lean, it is not impossible, and its benefits can be exceptionally rewarding.

The first rule of sustainability is to preserve our "natural capital," our finite natural resources, especially the soil, air, and water on which life depends. When we despoil those, we irrevocably reduce the ability of earth to support both present and future life.

In addition to natural capital, sustainability uses the concept of "natural income." Natural income is the resources that nature replaces daily in large quantities, mostly solar energy and derivatives from it, like wind and water power. Earth receives about 15,000 times more solar energy daily than all the energy we use in all forms. We just don't tap it effectively at the present time. Our fossil energy sources are merely stored versions of natural income; however, their supplies are finite, and burning fossil energy impacts our environment. Therefore, sustainability encourages organizations to reduce or eliminate reliance on fossil energy, replacing it with natural income energy. This will leave those marvelously complex hydrocarbons for future generations to use in other, creative ways. (And the economics are starting to favor renewable energy, because of the relentless increase in price of both oil and natural gas.)

The second rule of sustainability is to eliminate the release of toxic materials from our products and our processes. There is no "away" where we can throw them.

Despite progress, we have a long way to go toward reducing toxic disposal. In 2003, U.S. industry released only 4.4 billion pounds of reported chemicals, compared with 6.6 billion pounds in 2000.[6] That one-third reduction is a good start, but we're still dumping too much. These releases have a cumulative effect, like a slow accumulation of mercury in your body. In the four years, 2000–2003, the United States alone released 21.3 billions pounds of toxins; we have no idea how much we have released in the last 100 years. We have no idea how much other countries have released. We have no idea about the long-term effects these toxics may have, and pollution knows no boundaries. For example, the air in the U.S. now carries pollution from coal-burning power plants in China.

Sustainability is still relatively early in its adoption cycle, like Just-In-Time (the predecessor of lean) was in the 1980s. Predictably, companies fall into one of the following categories:

- Some ignore environmental and/or social regulations, hoping that no top manager assumes the role of CJO — Chief Jailable Officer.
- Most comply with regulations, seeing little benefit in doing more than is minimally required (as they did with quality thirty years ago).

- Some go beyond compliance, and are environmentally oriented and/or socially-oriented; these companies gain a green image, or benefit from being one of the 100 best companies to work for in the U.S.
- A small but growing number are seriously pursuing a true sustainability strategy.

Why Go for Sustainability?

However, from a long-term global perspective, a sustainable strategy is the best, and perhaps only, choice. For example:

If China used the same amount of oil per capita as the United States, it would consume the entire present world production of 83 million barrels a day. Even the most optimistic projections of oil production don't see it doubling, and some experts think we're very close to maximum production.

If everyone on earth lived to the U.S. level of consumption, we would require the resources of five planet earths. Western Europeans have basically the same standard of living, using only about half the resources per capita as Americans.

Earth's population has doubled since 1960, but the amount of arable land continues to decrease, and the world yield of five major grains is down fifteen percent since 1985.

The United Nations estimates that job-related deaths (accidents and illnesses) claim more than two million lives per year, and that number is rising.[7]

Finally, all the world religions view the earth as a gift from the creator of life, strongly implying that we should treat it respectfully.

We read such things with disbelief, as if from some other world, fearing to take action lest we plunge our company into a financial tailspin. On a planning horizon longer than a few budget cycles, it's obvious that something very different has to start happening, but to start pursuing sustainability, we usually need some nearer-term reasons. An organization's outlook broadens when it adopts the well-known triple bottom line: profit, people, and planet, rather than being financially directed toward a single stakeholder (the owners).

The quantifiable business benefits from a well-designed sustainability program fall into the following three classic categories.

<u>Reducing Operating Costs:</u> When done by eliminating waste, environmental improvement should also reduce cost unless the anomalies of the cost system mask the effect. For example:

Oki Semiconductor Manufacturing in Portland, Oregon, implemented one of the first ISO 14001 environmental management systems in the U.S.. After a year, its ongoing annual savings were double the out-of-pocket costs.

Baxter International saved $17,000 in three months by reducing water usage in one plant, with no capital investment. Its wastewater treatment plant no longer needed to expand.[8]

The Collins Companies, a wood-products company founded in 1855, reclaimed heat from ovens that cure hardboard coating. It saved $118,000 in electricity cost per year by installing a single, 300hp electric motor to replace six motors. Altogether, it saved an estimated $1 million in the first year of implementing sustainability principles.

Rejuvenation, America's largest manufacturer of period reproduction lighting, adopted more environmentally benign manufacturing processes. Results included:
- Higher quality products.
- Selling selenium, which had been a contaminant in their wastewater, to a reclaiming processor. This allowed them to recycle and reuse their water, dramatically reducing the amount of wastewater generated.
- An electrostatic spray system for lacquering reduced VOC emissions 60 percent, allowed them to use water-based coatings, and produced a more durable coating.

Likewise, companies that adopt socially friendly policies reduce operating costs due to lower employee turnover, and improve profitability due to their ability to attract and retain brighter and more creative employees (without having to pay a salary premium). For example, Jeff Swartz at Timberland believes that the idea of helping others will create a "more productive, efficient, loyal, and committed employee base, which in turn helps produce 'real' results."[9]

<u>Attracting and Retaining "Better" Customers:</u> A company focused on the Triple Bottom Line offers more than price/delivery/quality to potential customers and potential suppliers. Customers interested in more than price are better long-term partners. They have a lower credit risk and a better chance of enduring.

In global markets, U.S. companies can no longer assume that the U.S. sets environmental standards. Europe has become the leader, passing tough laws for a wide range of products, including chemicals, automobiles, electronics, tools, and cosmetics. All automobiles and electronics either manufactured or sold in Europe must be taken back by the manufacturer at their end of life! Cosmetics and chemicals must pass the "precautionary principle": they are assumed to be hazardous unless proven otherwise.[10] How long will U.S. consumers willingly lag the protections afforded Europeans?

Both Nike, a leading footwear manufacturer, and Norm Thompson, a leading Northwest retailer, are replacing conventional clothing with environmentally friendly clothing. Norm Thompson's initial product offering using organic cotton was so successful that it has expanded that product line.

Lumber companies in Oregon and the Oregon Department of Forestry are investigating the possibility of seeking environmental certification for Oregon forests, a green seal of approval that would help give them an edge in a highly competitive market.[11]

Reducing Risks: Companies that have embraced Corporate Social Responsibility ("CSR") have outperformed the broader stock market indices since the inception of the Dow Jones Sustainability Index. And market analysts are starting to realize that socially responsible businesses are lower risk than "profit-is-the-only-goal" businesses, which includes Enron and their ilk.

In its financial cost calculations in loan reviews, J.P. Morgan is including the risk of a company losing business to a competitor that has lower greenhouse-gas emissions.[12] And Swiss Re is starting to charge higher insurance premiums to companies that emit excessive greenhouse gases, because greenhouse gases cause global warming, which increases weather-related insurance claims.

Europe's precautionary principle for cosmetics requires that a chemical be proven safe before it can be used on the skin. Some U.S. cosmetics manufacturers, such as Revlon, voluntarily insure that all their products sold anywhere meet that standard. Others, such as Proctor and Gamble, produce products that only meet the standards in the market in which they are sold. How will American women react when they realize that companies knowingly sold them products that were deemed unsafe in Europe?[13] Are the companies with dual safety standards opening themselves to future lawsuits, reminiscent of the Ford Pinto lawsuits?

A company that embraces sustainability does not worry about increasingly stringent regulations. At times sustainability can mean the difference between receiving building permits and not receiving them. And sustainable companies are positioned to favor tighter environmental and social regulations that can seriously damage competitors. Imagine the positive public relations impact of a business that openly favors tighter environmental regulation.

The less quantifiable, but perhaps even more important, aspects of implementing sustainability include:

- Reputation management,
- Investor relations and access to capital,
- Learning and innovation, and
- License to operate.

Why Start Sustainability Now?

Sustainability is rapidly transitioning from a fringe, avant-garde practice to mainstream. Most Fortune 500 companies now have an executive in charge of sustainability. The early adoption phase is rapidly ending. Just like lean in the late 1980's, the companies that adopt sustainability now will enjoy a major, long-term competitive advantage in their industries, which will force the laggards to adopt it.

From Lean to Sustainability

A company familiar with lean will easily grasp sustainability. Lean works when individuals and teams throughout an organization start asking questions such as "How does this add value to the customer?" and "How can we do this better?" Lean works when those individuals and teams have the resources, time, and encouragement to identify opportunities, investigate them, and implement improvements. Lean works when management walks the talk.

Sustainability works the same way — the only difference is the decision-making criteria. Rather than focusing exclusively on the economic customer (the one who is buying our product or service), sustainability focuses on three bottom lines — profitability, people, and the planet. It focuses on the longer term, on life.

Like lean, Sustainability starts with educating people at all levels to see with different eyes, ask pointed questions, and make decisions based on sustainable criteria. It aligns efforts at all levels toward an easily-understood goal. It depends on, and rewards, the creativity of people at all levels. However, unlike lean, it taps much deeper into the powerful, deep-seated human desire to help our children and our children's children thrive. Norm Thompson's employees "feel good about working for a company that cares about the health of people and the planet. One said, 'I love this company. It stands for the right things — sustainability and work/life balance.'"[14]

When a company implements sustainability, its employees at all levels start receiving compliments from their neighbors and the community; they work for a company that cares. Few people have ever experienced such an influx of goodwill. Much more than lean, this is a powerful motivation to insure that sustainability produces the promised results.

Sustainability is a new mental model that spreads. When an organization teaches its employees how to use sustainability in their decisions at work, they take them home and use them in the community — in schools, volunteer organizations (Scouts, Little League, Rotary, Kiwanis, church, etc.), and in their own lives. They encourage government officials to start using sustainability in their decisions. More naturally than with lean, a company starts to have a substantial, positive impact on its community at almost no cost.

Extending the Tool Set

For a company that has started on its lean journey, moving toward sustainability is relatively easy. Many lean tools are easily adapted and extended for sustainability, as illustrated by the following examples.

Value Stream Mapping: Widely used in lean thinking to see a whole picture and decide where to focus improvement efforts, it readily extends to sustainability, especially to the environmental side. Just add appropriate metrics, such as hazardous material used/generated, water used, and energy used.
Work Teams: Just as in lean, work teams are the heart of sustainability — they do most of the thinking, the data gathering, the analysis, the idea generating, and the implementing. And work teams, by their very nature, implement the social side of sustainability.
5-S: For sustainability, some companies add a sixth S, "Safety" to classic 5-S, which implements the social side. A few add a seventh S, "Sustainability". However, this reduces sustainability to a tactical tool, rather than an overarching objective and compelling vision.
Analysis Tools: Teams focusing on sustainability can incorporate traditional lean analytical tools, such as Pareto charts, Ishikawa diagrams,

and the "5 why's" into their analyses. For example, hazardous material and releases of toxic substances can be analyzed as if they were process defects. As with correcting quality problems at the source, the preferred solution for hazardous materials is to eliminate the need to use them. If that can't be done, kaizen the usage, inventory, and handling to the minimum possible.

Additional Tools for Sustainability

Since one main objective of sustainability is to live within nature's income, use of key resources, such as materials and energy, must be monitored as processes are improved or redesigned. The preferred approach is a mass and energy balance on a process, an input–output analysis like chemical engineers perform with a chemical process. This can range from very simple to highly complex.

A "gray box" example of resource usage is shown in Figure 2. It is taken from carpet manufacturing at Interface, Inc., one of the environmental leaders of U.S. industry. To analyze the overall picture, it

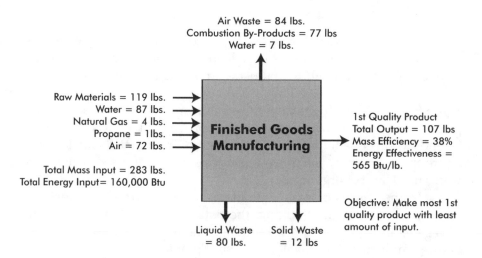

This figure is courtesy of Dave Gustashaw, Chief Engineer of Interface, Inc. Dave prepared it using data from Interface, Inc. and it is taken from slide 15 in Dave's presentation, "Applied Sustainability in Lean Operations," AME Conference 2005, Boston, MA.

Figure 2. Applied Sustainability: The Energy and Mass Balance of a Process

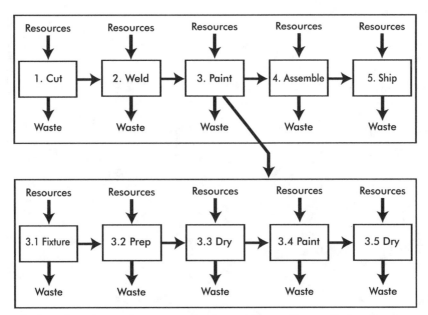

This hypothetical example assumes a bicycle manufacturer. The top diagram is a simplified breakdown of processes inside the overall gray box. The bottom diagram is a breakdown of processes in the paint department.

Figure 3. Breakdown and Simplification of the Gray Box

regards the entire process as a big gray box. Of course, subprocesses can be analyzed the same way with a mass–energy balance to come up with improvement ideas, subject to the usual problem of being able to measure the inputs and outputs, as shown in Figure 3.

To lean practitioners, Figure 4 looks more familiar. It is a Value Stream Map from Baxter Healthcare, modified to track the usage of just one material, water, in the production of a product line, rather than a complete mass/energy balance. Note that Baxter discovered that their product needed only 34 KL per day, but that they were consuming 300 KL per day, of which 201 KL went into the effluent waste stream. The opportunities were enormous; they were wasting 125,000 gallons of water per day.

Metrics make a vision become real in practice. Besides the metrics that usually guide lean operations, a few others are often associated with sustainability:

- Environmental:
    Energy used per unit of output
    Percent of energy from renewable resources

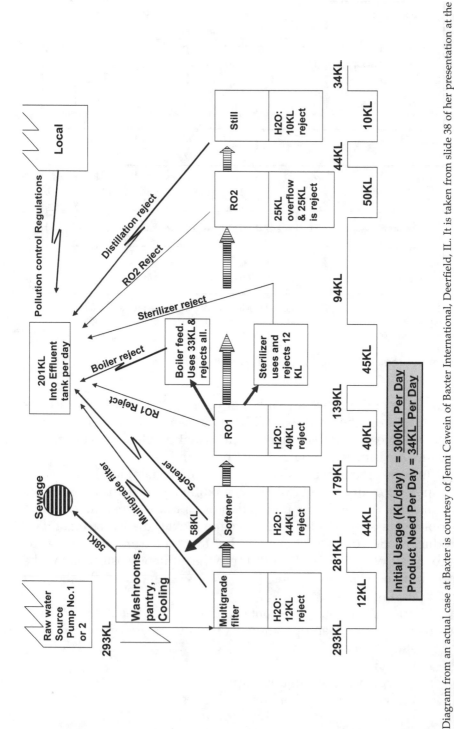

Diagram from an actual case at Baxter is courtesy of Jenni Cawein of Baxter International, Deerfield, IL. It is taken from slide 38 of her presentation at the 2005 AME Annual Conference, Boston, MA.

Figure 4. Value Stream Map Concentrating on Water Usage

Yield: Mass of finished goods from raw material consumed
Percent of raw materials reused or from recycled sources
Emissions, especially greenhouse gas emissions, both total
and per unit of output
Effluents discharged per unit of output
EPA(Federal)/DEQ (State) awards
TRI/SARA (toxic substances) reporting — number and names
of substances, and pounds used, discharged in waste, or lost,
both total and per unit of output
- Social/people
Percent of pension funded
Workplace safety — number of lost time accidents/year
Investment in people (education: number of hours of training
and education per person per year)
Rank in 100 best places to work
Number of product recalls in the last five years
Number of community service hours per employee
Employee turnover[15]

Costs, Paybacks, and Risks

From a business strategy viewpoint, sensibly starting down the sustainability path is a no-lose proposition, as shown in Figure 4. Of course, long-term, sustainability is something we all have to do, but companies worry about how it will affect the business in the next 5–10 years. Can a company risk being a sustainability leader?

| | | **Marketplace Regards Sustainability As...** | |
		Important	Unimportant
	Implement	**A. Big Win** Cost Savings Better customers Better employees Better suppliers	**B. Smaller Win** Cost Savings Better employees Better suppliers
Company → Strategy on Sustainability	**Don't Implement**	**C. Big Loss** No cost savings Lose best customers	**D. Neutral (delay)**

Figure 5. Should We Risk Being a Sustainability Leader?

Figure 5 is oversimplified. If a company's customers and investors expect it to be a sustainability leader, and it is not, its public relations black eye is not easy to fluff over. By contrast, a sustainability leader attracts environmentally-minded and socially-minded customers, employees, and investors. However, if the company is not really serious about sustainability, it may be accused of "greenwash."

But, as with lean, with an honest effort toward sustainability, a company attracts customers with similar values. It can also obtain better supplier partnerships, and if it must survive using more limited resources, it has a head start learning how to do so. The real risk is in being a sustainability laggard. For example:

- Lagging the marketplace in thought leadership, U.S. automobile manufacturers were caught without a line-up of offerings the market wanted to buy during the oil crisis in 1974, a situation that is starting to replay in 2005.
- "Also-ran" customers and suppliers will be forced to partner with other "also-rans."
- A lagging employer will have great difficulty attracting and retaining the best and brightest employees.
- A laggard will carry higher risk for insurance premiums, higher rates from financial institutions, higher risks from regulatory fines and penalties, and worst, higher risks of exclusion from markets that are strictly regulated.
- Laggards risk greater disruption if the cost and availability of raw materials and natural resources rises.

The major tactical question is how to prioritize sustainability compared to other initiatives, and whether it can be successfully implemented while other programs are also being implemented. Like lean, sustainability is a journey rather than a discrete project. Like lean, it requires more management leadership than financial investment.

Like lean, a major risk is the organizational impact of a "failed" implementation. Then risk-avoiders will hesitate to embrace a second effort at sustainability.

There are always potential technological risks — if a company pushes the state of the art, the result might be costly, or even a failure. However, most of the gains in a typical sustainability implementation carry little technological risk. For example, technological risks are very low from categorizing each chemical as red, yellow, or green, based on its toxicity, with the intention of phasing out all red chemicals. Working to reduce the waste of resources throughout the supply chain does not inherently require technological risk. Implementing an Environmental Management System, such as ISO 14001, does not require technological risk.

How to Start

Even more than lean, sustainability can start in an individual department of a company, then spread. Because sustainability is basically asking the right questions, balancing society, company profits, and the environment, many people inherently want to support it. It's not a "hard sell," except to overcome the assumption that it is economically unattractive.

For example, the U.S. Army now has embraced sustainability as a strategic initiative. But this initiative did not start at the top level, or even with military personnel. It began with a mid-level civil servant who read a book, then invited friends to start a book group, reading and discussing a book a month. Members of this group told others and gave them books to read. One such book recipient was the commander of a fort landlocked in a populous area, constantly criticized by the community for its impact on the environment, so he tried a pilot sustainability program. He and the community were both pleased with the results, so he told another base commander, who tried a pilot program with similar results, and the idea began to spread.

Sustainability works in organizations of all sizes, profit and nonprofit. It works in offices, stores, manufacturing plants, transportation companies, schools and universities, hospitals, and government at all levels. You can start asking the right questions in any operation, coach people on the tools, and then let the practice start to spread naturally.

Gary Langenwalter is a principal in ConfluencePoint, a Portland, OR consulting group specializing in creating the business and economic case for companies evaluating sustainability, then assisting them to successfully implement sustainability

Notes

1. Ayres, R.U., *Technology and Environment*, Washington, D.C., National Academy of Sciences, 1989.
2. Hawken, Paul, Amory Lovins, and L. Hunter Lovins, *Natural Capitalism: Creating the New Industrial Revolution*, New York, Little Brown, 1999, p. 52.
3. The definition is from the Bruntland Commission Report, United Nations, 1987.

4. Reingold, Jennifer, "Walking the Walk," *Fast Company,* November, 2005, pp. 82-83.

5. Arthur D. Little, *The Case for Corporate Citizenship,* 2002, http://www.adlittle.com/insights/studies/pdf/corporate_citizenship.pdf, p. 2.

6. From the U.S. EPA Toxic Release inventory at www.epa.gov/triexplorer/.

7. http://www.un.org/apps/news/story.asp?NewsID=14106&Cr=work&Cr1=safety, April 28, 2005.

8. Cawein, Jenni, and Rob Currie, "Turning Lean into Clean," AME Conference 2005, Boston, MA, p. 57.

9. Reingold, Jennifer, op. cit., p. 83.

10. Schapiro, Mark, "New Power for 'Old Europe'," *The Nation,* December 27, 2004, pp. 11-16.

11. Milstein, Michael, "Oregon might brand lumber with green seal of approval," *The Oregonian,* April 25, 2005, p. A1.

12. Carlton, Jim, "J.P. Morgan Adopts 'Green' Lending Policies," *Wall Street Journal,* April 25, 2005, p. B1.

13. Schapiro, op. cit., p. 13.

14. Owens, Heidi, and David Allaway, *Oregon Natural Step Network Toolkit,* Portland, Oregon, the Oregon Natural Step Network, 2003, Appendix A, p. 5.

15. For a complementary copy of a sustainability check sheet, contact Gary Langenwalter — glangenwalter@confluencepoint.org

Questions

Do you consider sustainability in designing your processes?

Which of your companies expenses could be reduced by focusing on sustainability? Water? Electricity?

Could a sustainable approach strengthen your customer base? Could it reduce risks?

Which lean approaches are you using that could be adapted for sustainability?

2

Lean Manufacturing and the Environment

Ignoring the 8th Deadly Waste[1]
Leaves Money on the Table

Mitch Kidwell

In Brief

Lean Strategies coincidentally benefit the environment, without the need for special "environmental" toolkits or a separate focus on environmental considerations, as explained by author Mitch Kidwell of the EPA.

Taking a break from a kaizen event, I had the rare opportunity to pick the brain of the sensei, a Japanese consultant who had been involved with lean manufacturing since before its arrival to the United States. Since I work for the Environmental Protection Agency (EPA), I asked him about the status of lean manufacturing in Japan, and in particular whether the focus of lean and efficient production had begun addressing environmental concerns. Through a few more questions and responses, his answer became clear. Environmental concerns are a part of the lean concept. Emissions to air and water, as well as the generation of solid/hazardous waste, represent a waste of production (i.e., no value to the customer), just as surely as the need for protective equipment (such as gloves and ear plugs) is, and that eventually lean would address them.

Lean usually helps the environment without really intending to. A Shingo Prize-winning study that EPA commissioned found that through Lean, many companies were saving money by taking steps that also benefited the environment, even when they were not consciously trying to do so. "Environmental" wastes, such as excess energy or water use, hazardous waste, or solid waste, present largely untapped opportunities to the lean practitioner. This is obvious if one steps back to consider the overall goals of lean manufacturing continually improving production efficiency. More efficient production means less energy used per unit produced. It means less material resources are used per unit produced, and materials (and energy, for that matter) are used or reused more efficiently. Aside from the obvious savings on production costs, this more efficient use means not only less energy and raw materials consumed, but also less material emitted to air and water, and less solid/hazardous waste generated. See the box for examples.

Examples of Environmental Gain from Production Process Kaizen

General Motors: An assembly plant evaluated paint booth cleaning operations; cleaning took place every other day. They discovered that the automated section of the painting operations only needed to be cleaned once a week, as long as the cleaning was thorough and bigger holes were cut in the floor grating to accommodate thicker paint accumulations. More efficient cleaning techniques and solvent recycling were also implemented.

Production gain:
Reduction in cleaning frequency reduced downtime and improved production flow.

Environmental gain:
Use of purge solvents was reduced by 3/8 gallons per vehicle.
VOC emissions from purge solvents were reduced 369 tons in the first year these modifications were implemented.

Goodrich Aerostructures: A facility shifted to lean point-of-use chemical management systems. Goodrich personnel worked with suppliers to get just-in-time delivery of chemicals in smaller, right-sized containers.

Production gain:
Delivery of right-sized containers to the point-of-use (either in work kits or by designated water spiders who courier materials to the point-of-use) reduced wasted worker movement and downtime.

(continued)

Therefore, EPA has begun to look very closely at lean as an area in which environmental and business practitioners can work together. On the one hand, lean practitioners save money finding undiscovered opportunities to eliminate the same wastes that concern environmental agencies. On the other hand, much expertise in environmental waste-minimizing opportunities already exists. It is readily available by tapping into the many years of knowledge that environmental experts and in-house Environment, Health, and Safety (EHS) personnel have in finding and eliminating wastes in ways that can significantly boost the economic bottom line.

Shifting to right-sized containers of chemicals reduced inventory and minimized the chance of chemicals expiring on the shelf.
Eliminated the need for four 5,000 gallon tanks containing methyl ethyl ketone, sulfuric acid, nitric acid, and trichloroethane, thus eliminating the need to address risk management planning and other chemical management requirements for the tanks.
Environmental gain:
Right-sized chemical containers reduced chemical use and hazardous waste generation. Minimized the waste generated through chemicals expiring in inventory.
Eliminating the four 5,000 gallon tanks eliminated the potential for large-scale spills.

The Gehl Company, West Bend, WI: The modification of a paint stripping process demonstrated the connection between lean manufacturing and pollution prevention — and demonstrated that pollution prevention saves money. (Or, in environmental lingo, "P2 Pays.") The company replaced chemical paint strippers with a blasting cabinet that uses small plastic particles to strip paint off parts.
Production Gain:
This directly resulted in savings of $32,000 a year in waste disposal costs.
Environmental Gain:
Employees had a safer and healthier work environment. The long-term expense or liability that this eliminated cannot be quantified, but it is "significant."

Please note that this type of process improvement and money-saving exercise was an EHS-oriented kaizen event, with the methodology being wholly consistent with lean manufacturing.

Environmental Waste: An Overlooked Savings Opportunity

Lean manufacturing first came to EPA's attention through case studies that demonstrated that very significant reductions in so-called "environmental wastes" (i.e., the 8th Deadly Waste) resulted from Lean activities solely focused on increasing production efficiency.[2] In 2003, EPA published this report, a collection of case studies of lean manufacturing activities and the environmental benefits that resulted. We are proud that this report won a Shingo Prize for research.

Companies usually do not consciously target "environmental" issues such as energy or water use, solid or hazardous waste, or chemical hazards, in their lean initiatives. Typically, environmental costs and impacts are considered overhead. Thus they tend to be hidden from the cost evaluation of a specific production process. (But with the recent rise in energy (and transportation) costs, an increasing number of companies have begun specifically targeting energy consumption for kaizen. Energy consumption has a very definite, measurable impact on a company's bottom line as well as a facility's environmental footprint.)

To understand Lean better, EPA began participating in actual kaizen events. That's how I met the sensei. When I suggested to him that the lack of environmental considerations during lean events was leaving opportunities for reducing costs on the table, he responded by saying that such a situation simply indicated a flaw in how lean was being implemented. He believed environmental considerations and the costs involved are an inherent component of lean. If cost-reduction opportunities concerning environmental wastes are being overlooked, then the true costs of production are not really being accounted for. He also went further by saying that if the true costs of production are not being overlooked, then it is likely a simple question of priorities.

He pointed out that many ideas for improving production efficiency reduce or eliminate all manner of wastes. Even if environmental wastes do not get first priority, it is likely that eventually lean will get around to addressing them. In some cases, this will happen through lean activities not intentionally focusing on environmental wastes, as was shown in EPA's 2003 report. However, companies may consciously choose to focus kaizen on particular "environmental" wastes.

Lean manufacturing confers very real benefits by reducing the costs of production and more efficiently using capital. If lean manufacturing also incorporates environmental considerations, it can help a company achieve many other long-term goals, such as environmental sustainability and maintaining a good relationship with the public.

Environmental Expertise Can Help Achieve Lean Goals

Lean manufacturing provides the opportunity for businesses to collaborate with EPA and other environmental agencies — either by working together directly to address a specific concern or by using environmental experts as a source of information and tools that lean practitioners can find helpful. For many years, EPA has promoted the concept of "pollution prevention," — eliminating pollution from the production process rather than installing costly "end of pipe" controls. Pollution prevention assistance providers have acquired years of expertise in finding ways to eliminate waste. They do audits with manufacturers, suggesting ways to save energy and reconfigure production processes to minimize the wastes generated, while at the same time, making the kinds of efficiency improvements that lean manufacturing also seeks out.

Most pollution prevention strategies actually save money. Few pollution prevention ideas would be voluntarily implemented if they only increased the cost of production. While the goal of pollution prevention is not to increase production efficiency per se, and the goal of lean manufacturing is not to minimize environmental wastes per se, both disciplines tend to arrive at the same, or at least consistent, end results.

From EPA's perspective, leveraging lean to achieve environmental goals is a no-brainer. Lean manufacturing represents the Rosetta stone for translating pollution prevention ideas into a language that makes sense to the operations side of a business. Likewise, focusing on environmental wastes can help companies achieve their lean goals.

EPA's "Lean and Environment" Initiative

To help bridge the gap, EPA has begun to observe how lean works in action, and to work with lean experts on strategies for targeting environmental wastes. EPA has partnered with several companies, Manufacturing Extension Partnerships (MEPs), and Federal facilities that have already begun making the connections between lean and the environment. We have been delighted to find that lean companies tend to be very free about sharing information, experience, expertise and the actual tools they've developed in furthering the goal of efficient production. We set about acquiring lean experience through attendance at lean conferences, workshops, visiting facilities to see firsthand the changes resulting from lean implementation, and by actively participating in kaizen events and other lean activities at various partner facilities. EPA participated in a special session at AME's 2005 conference in Boston and 2006 conference in Dallas, where EPA also had a booth.

Based on our experience and that of our partners, in January 2006, EPA developed and published "The Lean and Environment Toolkit" (see box copy). The Toolkit incorporates tools already developed and used by our partners, as well as new ideas that arose during our collaboration. Lean practitioners will find these tools to be very familiar; for the most part, they're traditional lean tools with slight adaptations to account for a slightly different perspective.

For example, the Toolkit includes a Value Stream Mapping (VSM) tool, which is basically the same as the traditional VSM, but adding a "starburst" to identify environmentally sensitive processes. These would be processes that involve the need for a permit, the use of hazardous materials, or where an opportunity for achieving environmental gains consistent with production efficiency is identified during the VSM exercise. Should such a process be addressed by a future lean event, the team working on the event would know to involve environmental, health, and safety (EHS) staff. More significantly, the Toolkit demonstrates how the VSM can also be adapted to track the use of raw materials, energy, or other utilities, such as water. Without adaptation, many lean techniques can also specifically address environmental concerns. They can be used in a kaizen event focused on a specific environmental problem, or in kaizen dealing with process waste in general.

Another fairly common example is a "6S Checklist" where "Safety" is the sixth "S." This checklist includes items for tagging potentially hazardous materials, and organizing them to minimize the risk of spills or unsafe exposure.

EPA has designated this Toolkit as "Version 1.0." In keeping with the continuous improvement philosophy, EPA expects to publish additional versions. We seek input on suggested changes, both in substance and presentation, to enhance the Toolkit's usefulness to lean practitioners. EPA welcomes suggestions for other lean concepts that EPA should pursue to enhance the environmental benefits of lean manufacturing. We seek information or data from you that EPA can provide to other companies to assist them in drawing their own links between Lean and

---

The Lean and Environment Toolkit

How can EPA help save you money? "The Lean and Environment Toolkit," published in January 2006, presents slightly modified standard lean tools, such as VSM and 5S, to include environmental considerations. The Toolkit also provides checklists and other standardized forms used during kaizen events that provide a framework for environmental considerations.

The Toolkit is available for download at www.epa.gov/lean. There is also a link on this site to provide comments, suggestions, and especially if you would like to share success stories involving lean manufacturing and its impact on the environment, or seek further information.

---

the environment.

EPA's lean website provides a link to make such suggestions. We really want to hear from you. Please contact us at www.epa.gov/lean. Bringing EHS into the Lean World.

A key recommendation in the Toolkit is to involve EHS staff more fully in Lean activities, and to draw on their environmental expertise. Currently, when EHS personnel are involved, their role is geared heavily toward health and safety, as well as ensuring compliance with OSHA requirements.

Environmental concerns are often downplayed, or even absent from kaizen activities. This seems to be a natural outgrowth of regarding environmental issues as a "monument" during kaizen, being cautious making changes to a production cell that may make perfect sense, but that would require a permit modification to maintain compliance, for example. But such environmental monuments are little different from other monuments that kaizen teams feel compelled to "lean around." Sooner or later they need to be addressed.

While compliance issues are rightfully a major concern, and people acknowledge that it's better to get such issues out in the open early in a kaizen event, there's still a natural inclination to downplay or even exclude environmental monuments from improvement considerations. As a result, EHS personnel participating in a kaizen event may leave their "environmental hat" behind, or be reluctant to offer their "environmental" ideas, believing that they will not receive full consideration because they come from "the nay-sayer."

However, more and more experienced lean companies are finding that it pays to encourage EHS personnel to wear their environmental hat. With that hat come insights into costs that are otherwise hidden from the operations side, and from the accounting system, but that's another issue. These insights can help evaluate the true costs associated with a particular production process, and find opportunities otherwise unseen.

For example, EHS staff are more likely to realize that a more expensive, but less toxic solvent may actually be more cost-effective if it results in less hazardous waste (or even none) being generated. The costs to treat and dispose of wastes often exceed the added expense of less toxic solvent.

Another all too common example is that it seems more efficient from a production perspective to combine wastewater streams and treat all the wastewater together. However, if one stream results in a hazardous waste, combining it with other wastewater streams can generate a much larger volume of hazardous waste. How could that happen? Suppose electroplating rinse water is one of the wastewater streams. Under the hazardous waste regulations, the sludge from the treatment of electroplating rinsewater is a hazardous waste. Combining the electroplating rinsewater with other wastewater streams does not change the regulatory status of the rinsewater (i.e., it remains electroplating rinsewater). So the sludge resulting from the treatment of the combined waste stream continues to be considered the sludge from the treatment of electroplating rinsewater, and so continues to be a hazardous waste, only now with a much larger volume because of the precipitants contributed by all the other wastewater streams. In such a situation, the added cost of treatment and disposal of the larger volume of hazardous waste could easily exceed the operational savings of combining all the facility's wastewaters, something an EHS person would know.

Combining waste streams can also adversely impact the recyclability of all resulting waste, impacting the cost of a facility's overall waste management program. For example, scrap metal and used oil are both recyclable, but combining the two could render both unrecyclable unless they are again separated. Even then, they are less attractive to a recycler. Too often, such environmental costs are hidden in overhead, and the insights that would have brought them to light during a kaizen event never arise if environment expertise is omitted or discouraged during the event.[3]

We strongly encourage companies to involve EHS staff in kaizen events on production processes, and encourage them to wear their "environmental hat." Certainly, many kaizen events do not require environmental insights. But with a little time and experience, managers soon learn when to involve EHS staff, just as they sense when to involve people from marketing, purchasing, or IT when a process kaizen is apt to cross boundaries. Unless they do, they'll never know what insights they missed.

Working Together Toward Sustainability

EPA has recognized that "lean strategies" coincidentally benefit the environment. As noted earlier, EPA also recognizes that lean is first and foremost a business model. Trying to hijack it to redirect to other goals will not be successful either for EPA or our business partners. Thus, we encourage targeting environmental wastes not for altruistic reasons, but because it serves the same goals as targeting wasted time, wasted motion, and other traditional "deadly wastes."

Nevertheless, the environmental benefits that result from kaizen activities can be quite significant. They can lead a company towards sustainability and a reputation as a good corporate citizen. Increasingly, companies concerned with their public image have adopted, directly or indirectly, the goal of reducing their environmental footprint in their mission statements. For a variety of reasons, they are taking steps well beyond what is required by law and looking at the "triple bottom line" of economic, environmental and social concerns. (Interested readers may want to review Gary Langenwalter's article "'Life' is Our Ultimate Customer: From Lean to Sustainability" in *Target*'s first 2006 issue.[4])

While not every company is ready for this step, EPA encourages companies to consider it, and views the lean journey as an excellent way to start the environmental journey.

EPA's goal is to maximize the environmental benefits of lean by raising the awareness of the linkage between lean and the environment. We are developing pollution prevention and other relevant expertise. We will develop informational materials, such as the Toolkit, when appropriate. To do this, EPA needs the input of lean companies. We need you to tell us what we can do to help your company continue the lean path. We trust that environmental considerations can become incorporated as an inherent part of lean, without the need for special "environmental" Toolkits or a separate focus on environmental considerations. We need not wait for lean to eventually address environmental considerations — they are worth considering now as part of efficient production.

Mitch Kidwell is a senior staff person in EPA's National Center for Environmental Innovation (NCEI). Prior to that, he spent fourteen years in EPA's hazardous waste regulatory program.

References

1 The 8th Deadly Waste is a term coined by lean manufacturing companies and assistance providers that have partnered with EPA in pursuing the goal of enhancing the environmental benefits inherent in lean manufacturing. "Environmental waste" is a term used to distinguish between those emissions and solid/hazardous wastes that EPA typically considers waste from the 7 Deadly Wastes associated with lean manufacturing.

2 "Lean Manufacturing and the Environment: Research on Advanced Manufacturing Systems and the Environment and Recommendations for Leveraging Better Environmental Performance," EPA100-R-03-005, October 2003. This EPA publication is available for downloading at http://www.epa.gov/lean/leanreport.pdf.

3 For smaller companies that do not have such compartmentalization of key functions, insights into environmental costs and alternative processes and materials can often be gained through pollution prevention assistance providers, Manufacturing Extension Partnerships (MEPs), State regulatory agencies, or private consultants that specialize in such issues.

4 "'Life' is Our Ultimate Customer: From Lean to Sustainability," by Gary Langenwalter, *Target*, Volume 22, Number 1, p5.

Questions

Do you devote considerable time and expense to cleaning operations? Do those operations produce hazardous wastes?

Could you reduce the quantities of hazardous materials on hand?

Could you reduce waste disposal costs through a focus on sustainability?

Do you regularly interact with the EPA? Have you discussed lean strategies with them?

3

Sustainable Development

How DuPont Seeks to Increase Shareholder
and Societal Value, Decrease Its Footprint
Along the Entire Value Chain

Dawn Rittenhouse

In Brief

At DuPont, sustainability is an official corporate goal driving strategies and tactics. In this article, Dawn Rittenhouse of DuPont describes the company's efforts to carry out corporate policy and produce real benefits.

DuPont defines sustainable growth as creating shareholder value and societal value while decreasing our footprint throughout the value chain. We define our footprint as injuries, illnesses, incidents, waste, emissions and depletable forms of raw material and energy.

Our journey to become a sustainable company began in 1989. Before that, DuPont was focused on complying with all laws and regulations wherever we operated. The one differentiated area was worker safety. Since DuPont's founding in 1802, the company operated on the premise that all injuries are preventable. An effective management system was in place to set goals, measure and reward progress, and understand underlying issues.

When Ed Woolard became the CEO in 1989, he used his first speech to emphasize the need for environmental stewardship and coined the phrase, "Corporate Environmentalism." Thanks to this strong focus, the company established a set of goals for the year 2000 that included targets like 90 percent reduction in air carcinogens, 70 percent reduction in air toxins, 50 percent reduction in packaging waste to landfill, and elimination of deepwelling of hazardous wastes. At that point, an Environmental Committee of the board of directors

27

was established as well as a Corporate Business Council involving senior leadership from the corporation.

In 1993, the Environmental Committee of the board of directors challenged DuPont to revise the Safety, Health and Environmental Policy to better align with the actual strategy of the company. Following a year-long process which involved many people within the company as well as external thought leaders, the new Safety, Health and Environmental Health Commitment was endorsed by the board and signed off by all the senior corporate leadership. The significant steps in the commitment were 1) the goal of zero injuries, illnesses, incidents, waste, and emissions; and 2) employee accountability for meeting the commitment.

Challenge to Minimize Risk and Environmental Impact

When Chad Holliday became the CEO in 1998, he took the next step by establishing sustainable growth as DuPont's overriding objective. The challenge to corporate leaders is to fulfill the needs of a growing world population using the best forms of technology while minimizing risk and environmental impact. This challenge brings up many questions: Do the businesses and technologies that the company is building lend themselves to sustainable models? What actions must DuPont take now to make sure that the company is able to maintain sustainable growth in the new century?

Chad Holliday is also applying his leadership in a broader capacity. In 1999 he was elected as the chairman of the World Business Council for Sustainable Development (WBCSD, www.wbcsd.org) for the years 2000–2001. In addition, he assumed co-chair responsibility for a working group focused on sustainability through the market. In 2001, the working group's final report was launched during the Commission for Sustainable Development meeting at the United Nations.

Keys to Success

Corporate success in adopting a sustainable development growth model depends on these elements:

- *Sustainable growth linked to the core values of the company.* DuPont's core values are safety and environmental stewardship, enhancing the lives of employees and the communities in which we operate, integrity and high ethical standards; and treating people fairly and with respect, consistent with the key elements of sustainable development.

- *A business purpose for pursuing sustainable growth.* Every business has to be able to see sustainability as an opportunity for real growth, not as a kind of corporate philanthropy or do-gooder enterprise.
- *Guidelines that help to incorporate sustainable growth into business strategies.* Strategic pathways have to be identified to enable progress toward sustainability and simultaneously advance traditional measures of business growth. Tools like life cycle analysis and risk analysis are also available to help businesses understand their impacts.
- *The ability to measure whether or not we are becoming more sustainable.* A quantifiable metric had to be applicable across our businesses so we do not have to rely on descriptive measures or depend on anecdotes. Our goals for 2010 are shown in Figure 1. Figure 2 reflects DuPont's environmental progress.
- *A means for demonstrating to ourselves and to our stakeholders that progress toward sustainable growth would be central to creating value.* Since 1992, DuPont has published a Progress Report to communicate with employees and our stakeholders about our progress. In 1999, we created an integrated report that included economic, social, and environmental progress.

Greater Expectations

Translating these goals into day-to-day activities means realigning our strategies. We made it the expectation of our businesses that they need to incorporate sustainable growth goals into their operating plans. Once a year, the vice president of safety, health, and environment (SHE) meets with senior business leaders to review their plans and

Goals for 2010
- Hold total energy usage flat at 1990 levels
- Reduce global greenhouse gas emissions by 65 percent from a 1990 base.
- Source ten percent of energy from renewable resources
- Generate 25 percent of revenues from non-depletable resources.

Figure 1.

progress. The CEO also asks operating groups about their performance in integrating these goals into their businesses.

For example, our Engineering Polymers business which makes polymers used in automotive and other applications set a goal of zero polymer waste to landfills. Such programs may be developed at the business unit level (Lycra®, Nylon, Polyester Films, etc.), or tailored to individual operations and local community needs. For instance, at the Kinston, NC site, reducing impacts on the local aquifer was a concern, so a site-specific plan for reducing water use was developed.

Each year, all the businesses submit plans into the Corporate Environmental Plan database. This process enables corporate leadership to determine the most cost-effective way to spend resources for needed improvements — reducing emissions in one business 100 percent and 80 percent in another versus having each business reduce 90 percent and saving the corporation millions of dollars.

A small percentage of every employees' compensation is affected by performance against SHE goals. Pay at risk is evaluated in terms of traditional economic measures like return on net assets, earnings, cash flow, safety, health, and environmental performance.

Business Purpose

We can plan and implement programs designed for environmental, safety and social benefit; however, to be sustainable, we know that our

	1990	2000(est.)	% Change
Air carcinogens	9.1	1.1	88
Priority air	68.0	18.0	74
Greenhouse gases	24.6	10.2	59
Deepwell disposal	166.0	30.0	82
TRI releases	225.0	55.0	75
TRI as generated	890.0	550.0	38
Hazardous waste	2750.0	1650.0	40
TRI+ Toxic release inventory			

Figure 2. DuPont Environmental Progress

programs must also make business sense. We need to ask ourselves the question, "What can we do to make these improvements, and find competitive advantage?" You need to evaluate the real business value of products that have less impact.

For example, one of our former businesses developed an alternative way to develop film, replacing a suspect carcinogenic chemical in this operation. We could have competed head-to-head in the market against the incumbent product, with our "green" offering. However, we believed that we could be much more successful if we developed a holistic approach to our customers. The customers collect all the chemicals used in processing film, which were returned in the original containers to our plant. We removed silver residuals, credited customers for the value of the silver, and then recycled the chemicals. You need to think about costs in your operation, but more importantly, consider your customer's cost and concerns. If you are thinking holistically and taking customers, suppliers, and end users' needs into consideration, you will be generating new opportunities that make business sense and reducing impacts throughout the value chain.

Closer Ties with Customers

We are finding better ways to listen to our customers' needs, and to anticipate what products and services will help them to improve their competitiveness through sustainable development. DuPont, for example, manufactures nylon fiber used in carpet, or floor coverings. Ten years ago, when we were asking ourselves how to make the business more successful, we recognized that approximately two billion pounds of carpet was thrown away each year. We started asking how we could make the industry more sustainable and improve our business success. We developed a series of initiatives tied into the business. One was to look at the fiber part of the business. We sold white fiber to carpet manufacturers primarily located in Dalton, GA where it was dyed and manufactured into carpet. It takes a lot of water to dye fiber and causes a heavy load on the public water treatment facilities.

We asked if we could make a business case for pre-dyeing the fiber as part of our fiber processing. There would be little waste or emissions if this step were handled in our polymer process. After discussions with our customers, we developed a line of pre-dyed fibers, which was very well accepted. Now we are the largest producers of pre-dyed fibers. The change required many adjustments in our processes related to inventory management and production planning, to avoid carrying a large inventory of various colors and deniers (a measure of thickness). This process has required us to work more closely with customers; we need to know what they need, and when. Our closer ties with customers allow us to operate almost on a Just-In-Time basis.

An extension of this closer focus on customers is our downstream involvement with designers and others who select and manage the installation and maintenance of carpet in commercial applications such as hotels. We developed DuPont Flooring Systems as a complete carpet service to commercial customers. We help to design the carpet, plan for delivery so the timing is right, and arrange for the installation. Our installers are DuPont employees. We've worked on the special safety issues for carpet installers, reducing the injuries experienced by many people working in the field (many carpet installers use their knee as a hammer to stretch the carpet tight, causing long-term injuries). These safety efforts not only reduce our workmen's compensation costs as injuries were reduced, but also help us to attract employees. Our sales force also works with customers to provide proper carpet cleaning and maintenance. This service extends the life of the product — a benefit to the environment, and a cost savings to the customer.

We also have a recycling facility in Chattanooga, TN. They remove the nylon face on carpet and sell it to our polymers business for use in Engineering Polymers applications like car parts. We have found uses for all the other parts of the installed carpet — padding, etc. One of the longer-term challenges for the flooring industry is to design carpets so they are easier to disassemble and recycle.

We work with customers so they understand their cost through the whole life cycle of the carpet. We've made progress in this area of the business, but we continue to look for ways to reduce our footprint by making carpets more recyclable as well as develop fibers that offer increased value to customers. Eventually we hope to refine the process so that recycled nylon can go back into more demanding technical products. We are looking at more cost effective ways to use recycled material in artificial turf, for example.

This focus on customers can be applied in many areas, throughout the value chain. Look at the key issues your customers have, and look for ways you can provide value by using your knowledge; for example, offering a customer pre-dyed material to reduce cost and minimize their impact on water treatment facilities.

Another win-win example is our work with [...]
paint operations. We provide complete car pai[...]
Oakville, ON plant. We began working together o[...]
years ago. Ford came to us, noting that they wan[...]
want to sell paint. They wanted to leverage our kn[...] ...
venting flaws, good coverage, etc. We worked out a process so that
DuPont employees located at the Ford facility manage the paint operation including buying the primers and paint. There was a major program just to develop this partnership. We had to work together to
understand what it costs to paint a car. There were issues about our
workers at a Ford operation; safety, health, and environmental standards needed to be discussed and agreed on. The new relationship
started in 1996. It's been a win-win situation. Ford gains lower prices,
and DuPont's lower paint volumes were offset by improved efficiencies. The result is a 50 percent reduction in VOC (volatile organic compounds) emissions.

It is something any business can think about: selling the function,
not just the product.

Partnership/Supply Chain Issues

We are working with key customers and suppliers to broaden our sustainable development work. Each business in DuPont is required to do
product reviews on a two-, three-, or four-year cycle depending on the
risks associated with the product. We are now working with customers
and suppliers in those reviews to consider the cradle-to-grave, or
hopefully the cradle-to-cradle issues — in other words, what they are
doing, and what we are doing, and how we can create better solutions.
Some of our customers have taken the lead, and we are taking steps.
For example, the automotive OEMs have quality standards and certification processes that encompass these issues.

As a supplier to Nike, we are working to provide materials as they
try to develop a more sustainable shoe — extending the life of the shoe
and making it more recyclable. We are also in discussion with other
companies — consumer, automotive, and flooring companies — to
understand key issues in the value chain and to design new products
which are more sustainable.

Our internal communications and team work also involves many
people. People who design new products, management and manufacturing, and others who work with marketing to improve our sustain-

development initiatives. We need business people involved; it doesn't do any good to design a product unless it makes business sense.

A team of employees in Europe created a peelable lid system for packaging applications that eliminates solvent emissions from lacquer coatings, reduces packaging materials, and improves taste and odor impartation. This effort has gained DuPont a ten percent share of the lidding market and reduced 1000 tons of methyl acetate solvent per year in Europe.

Packaging is another key area where we can reduce impacts by partnering with customers and suppliers. In our agricultural chemical business in Brazil, for example, we had a team that worked aggressively on packaging issues. Through better packaging design and increased packaging line productivity, the business cased over $340,000 per year and reduced packaging waste by more than 100 tons. This teamwork helped us to improve our performance in reducing packaging waste across the board consistent with our 1990 goal for reduced packaging waste going to landfills from customers. We reduced our packaging waste level by over 50 percent before 2000.

We also had a joint team which created a new process for terathane production, a precursor to Lycra. By coordinating the work at our European and U.S. sites, we figured out how to reduce materials usage in this process by four million pounds a year. This change also increased our earnings $4 million a year. Despite some differences in these locations, our sustainable development teamwork prevailed.

We are continuing to refine our expectations with suppliers in line with our SHE goals. We ask about their policies and their progress. With over 10,000 suppliers around the world, we have obviously developed much closer partnerships with some companies than with others. What we focus on is how we use material, and learning how we can work together more effectively to support customer needs.

The challenge of how to work on the whole value chain is critical. We can work inside our own gates, but if the value chain is not sustainable, then over the long term, we will not have a business. It's going to require different working relationships, different ways of working within the value chain. We've hardly scratched the surface in this area. What we are looking for are more pilots, where we have purchasing, sales, and others engaged in this process. The challenge is that in the short term it is much easier to just work on a price; changing your process or the ways you work with customers and suppliers takes a lot of up front work.

There are many training opportunities and many organizations share information on sustainable development. It's important to get out and see what other companies are doing. Find customers or suppliers with successful projects, and then get started on a project. Your stakeholders will find it easier to buy in, to see that their business is valued, if you invest in learning about their processes and ways to make improvements in sustainable development.

Research and Development Projects

Existing products as well as new products require this holistic approach. Key areas to be considered for research and development projects as part of our stewardship and sustainable growth assessment process are:

1. Understand the product trail including major impacts from suppliers, customers, users, and final disposition.
2. Determine global inventory listing status for product and key raw materials.
3. Determine if human and environmental toxicity studies are necessary.
4. Understand risk characterization including exposure potentials; implement plans to minimize any exposure potentials.
5. Understand occupational health risks; implement plans to minimize them.
6. Determine and characterize waste and emissions associated with the product; implement plans to minimize.
7. Assess energy use, material efficiency, and water use; implement plans to minimize usage.
8. Determine if the product can be reused or recycled.
9. Develop plans to optimize packaging.
10. Develop material safety data sheets and labels for each country where the product will be sold.

Metrics: More Than Safety Data Sheets

Life cycle risk analysis, as part of our product stewardship program, also requires critical attention. We understand that much more than safety data sheets must be considered. We ask, "How are we making our products and offerings more sustainable? How are these concerns integrated into new product development?" We must learn which materials are hazardous, how much energy and water usage results from manufacture and use of a product, and how to make the best use of databases and other tools to minimize impacts.

There is no single measure encompassing all of these concerns. What we have tried to do is use a metric that looks at shareholder value-added per pound of product. Are we creating more value without making a lot more "stuff"? We are learning to evaluate the knowledge intensity of our products. Instead of building a new plant to make more product, and using more materials and petroleum resulting in more shipments to landfills, we need to learn how our knowledge can help us to reduce environmental and other impacts. How do we design circular systems to reuse materials, looking at creating value in a broader sense — not just as creating more product?

Knowledge Sharing, Recognition

Sharing information about sustainable development innovation and experience is a high priority. One of the ways that DuPont encourages this process is through our annual competition in this area. A team of internal and external judges recognize 12 winners from around the world in the competition. Our chairman hosts the awards ceremony. Winners receive trophies and their teams also get $5000 which they can contribute to a charity in the community where they work. About 60 candidates are considered by the corporate panel but more than 400 nominations are originally submitted for consideration. Details of the entries are available through our intranet for DuPont employees; our corporate website, www.dupont.com lists winners.

Several entries for the years 1999 and 2000 included:

- Thanks to teamwork in the company's global Polyester Films business, we reduced waste generation throughout our value chain by decreasing the number of components used in packaging, reusing as many of the components as possible, and recycling the materials at the end of their useful life. Results during the past four years include keeping more than 30 million pounds of film packaging at customer locations out of landfills, helping customers with disposal challenges, and reducing packaging costs by $7.6 million.
- In our Fluoroproducts operation in the Netherlands, a team created and launched a thermal system to convert gaseous fluorocarbon waste to saleable aqueous hydrogen fluoride. Their successful project helped DuPont avoid a $5 million end of pipe treatment investment, trimmed our external disposal costs $600,000 by

handling another waste stream from Fluoropolymers in the same facility, and decreased the equivalent of 12 billion pounds of carbon dioxide emissions per year.

- Individual efforts make a difference too, as demonstrated by Weber da Silva Lobo in our Crop Protection business in Brazil. He created a process to convert a solid chlorinated organic residue into commercial products (propanil and 3,4 dichloro aniline). His accomplishments eliminated $10 million in residue storage and incineration costs.

- Sabine, TX Nylon business employees Elizabeth F. Longoria and Marc G. Saenz significantly decreased benzene and other organic emissions during cleaning and turn-around procedures. They devised a carbon-filled porous mat that is placed over trenches and equipment openings during equipment cleaning and maintenance procedures. Workers can avoid prolonged use of breathing protection, flammable vapors are no longer present in the atmosphere, and workers can enter the area immediately (since normal work activities can resume faster, the innovation boosts uptime).

We also avoid reinventing the wheel by using many networks within the company. A representative from each business meets on a regular basis with others who share information about key aspects of sustainable growth. We communicate by email, sharing best practices. Product stewardship is another network that meets several times a year, in addition to transportation, waste and emissions, and process safety management. Presentations may represent internal improvement projects, or we may have external presenters, such as a representative from other organizations.

We learn from external sources as well. Trading experiences about sustainable development's successes is one of the benefits from participation in the World Business Council for Sustainable Development (www.wbcsd.org). The Global Environmental Management Initiative (GEMI) is another organization sponsoring a sustainable development group which has identified key elements of best in class practices (www. Gemi.org). Each of these organizations has reports available to the public, plus members-only databases. The website for *Tomorrow* magazine (www.tomorrow-web.com) offers information and contacts in the sustainable development arena. For example, an article featured in the magazine's April/May 2001 issue, "Eco-Surf's Up," noted winners versus time-wasters among related websites.

Willingness to Learn

The goal of sustainable development requires commitment and action. Change can be uncomfortable. Yet most stakeholders are really interested in helping to improve a company's performance. The adversarial stuff disappears pretty quickly when you can demonstrate a case for change and progress. We need to be willing to make changes, not to be defensive about what we are already doing. Stakeholders need to understand that many times because of capital or other restraints, we cannot change our products or process immediately, so transition strategies have to be developed.

Most companies have great business stories; improving yield, for example, often is accompanied by gains in environmental and safety performance. We've learned that we need to go out and get some successes under our belt, and then build on this success to show benefit in social, environmental, economic, and other areas. Communication is essential. Let others know of your successes, and more people want to get involved — employees, customers, and suppliers, and others along the entire value chain.

It is a learning experience, one that absolutely requires top leadership involvement and support. Sustainable development reflects a higher purpose than just making money.

Sustainable growth is a journey and we are just at the beginning of this work, but we are on the path of trying to figure it out. DuPont will soon be 200 years old. We believe that we must integrate sustainability into our businesses to thrive for another 200 years.

Dawn Rittenhouse is DuPont's director of sustainable development. Within DuPont she works with the business units to help them integrate sustainability strategies into the business planning processes. She is co-chair of a sustainable development group within the Global Environmental Management Initiative (GEMI) and co-chair of a working group on Innovation and Technology for the World Business Council for Sustainable Development (WBCSD).

Questions

Does your company have a formal statement of environmental commitment? Is sustainable growth linked to the core values of your company?

Do you measure whether your company is becoming more sustainable? Do you have specific goals related to sustainability?

Is employee compensation tied to performance against goals of sustainability?

Do you work with customers and suppliers on sustainability issues?

Is sustainability considered in product development?

4

Reverse Logistics Provides Green Benefits

Ray Kulwiec

In Brief

Global attention and commitment to environmentally-friendly operations encompasses reverse logistics. In this article, author Ray Kulwiec explores related initiatives by Coors Brewing Company and Dell. Reverse logistics is much more than a means of handling returns and recovering/reusing discarded parts; it extends to design and other elements of the product's life cycle. Incentives for environmental performance improvement, in addition to ethical and regulatory concerns, often include financial benefit as well.

No longer just a way to handle returns, reverse logistics provides an environmentally-friendly method of recovering and reusing parts and materials after a product's life cycle has ended. In many cases it can also add "green" to the bottom line.

In Japan, any products purchased by the government must, by law, have a specific content of recycled materials.

In the Netherlands, manufacturers are held responsible for the collection, processing, and recycling of used products such as refrigerators, washers, freezers, TVs, and consumer electronics items and their associated packaging.

In the European Union (EU), a directive on handling waste from electrical and electronic equipment has been issued and member states are working on national legislation to implement it.

In the United States, there are hundreds of environmental laws and regulations within individual states, as well as the federal government, which include mandates for recycling operations and responsibility for packaging recovery. However, more research is needed, and a more clear-cut and comprehensive approach needs to be established.

Environmentally-friendly manufacturing and distribution operations are growing in many parts of the world. There are three driving forces for this trend: 1) environmental laws and regulations are increasingly widespread, 2) consumers are becoming receptive to products made from recycled as well as virgin materials, and 3) some companies are finding recycling, remanufacturing, and processing of used products, materials, and packaging to be good business that represents additional sources of revenue.

The Reverse Logistics Approach

A major weapon in the fight against environmental damage is reverse logistics. One view of reverse logistics is the handling of "returns," especially in such areas as TV shopping, retail, and mail-order operations. Certainly some operations of this type have a significant percentage of returns, and often separate systems are set up for dealing with returned merchandise and its reuse and resale.

Today, reverse logistics takes on a broader scope. It involves recycling and reuse of materials contained in a product and its packaging, after that product's useful life has ended. Reverse logistics is a departure from landfilling or incinerating used-up materials — practices that are no longer acceptable in many situations. In place of landfilling or incineration, reverse logistics includes recycling, material substitution and reuse, and remanufacturing. It takes in all the logistics steps involved in collecting, disassembling, and processing used products, parts, materials, and packages to provide an environmentally safe method of recovery (see Figure 1).

To be successful, reverse logistics must encompass the entire supply chain. Trading partners have to work together to ensure that the reverse logistics process is linked across all levels of the chain.[1]

The European Example

Europe has long had a strong and vocal "green" movement. Today that movement has been translated into specific mandates that manufacturers will have to follow in order to do business in Europe. A leading country in this regard is the Netherlands, which adopted reverse logistics legislation in 1999.

Under the Dutch program, manufacturers must not only develop a plan for manufacturing and distributing products, but must also

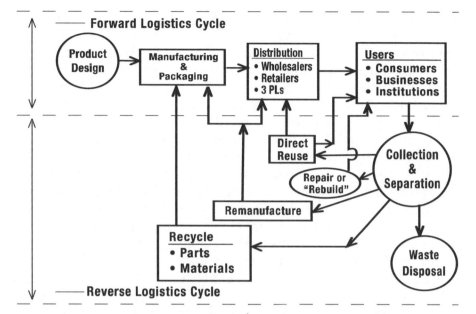

Figure 1. Reverse logistics is performed after a product's useful life has ended. It involves recovery of parts and materials from outdated or used-up products, with an eye toward protecting the environment. In some cases a product may still be directly reusable, after some cleaning or minor adjustment. In other cases, products and their components are totally unusable, and are disposed of as waste. However, a large proportion of used products and parts can be rebuilt, remanufactured, or recycled back for use in manufacturing the same product or different products. An ideal is integrating forward and reverse logistics cycles together into a closed-loop system.

plan for the eventual recycling and reuse of those products and their components after the last user has disposed of them (that is, after their primary life cycle has ended). This planning process may go all the way back to designing the product for ease of disassembly and recyclability. In any case, producers (manufacturers) and importers have final "producer responsibility" for the collection, processing, and recycling of both "white goods" (such as refrigerators, coolers, freezers, washing machines, and hair dryers) and "brown goods" (such as TVs and loud speakers).[2] Typically, the actual collection is performed on a fee arrangement by retailers and municipalities. Consumers do not incur a cost.

A typical logistics path may be the following: Used goods may be picked up from the user by a retailer. The used product is then picked up from the retailer's distribution center by a third-party logistics provider (3 PL), and delivered to a processor. The processor then removes harmful substances, disassembles and separates parts and materials, and sells these parts and materials to firms specializing in remanufacturing products using these contents. Processors are required to attain a recycling rate of 75 percent; that is, 75 percent of the total weight of the collected, discarded goods must be made available for reuse. Other related logistics paths may include use of municipal depots or regional transshipment stations.[3]

Following the Dutch example, the EU has issued a directive on waste from electrical and electronic equipment (WEEE). The directive sets criteria for the collection, treatment, recycling, and recovery of WEEE. It makes producers (manufacturers) responsible for financing most of these activities. Householders can return WEEE at no cost.

Currently many EU member states are working on national legislation to implement the terms of the directive. The United Kingdom, for example, is performing a total review at this writing, with a final implementation plan expected to be available later in 2006. A major issue is how to promote environmental benefits without placing undue financial burden on producers.[4]

Reverse Logistics Research

Research on reverse logistics is being conducted in Europe by teams from the following universities: Erasmus University (Rotterdam, The Netherlands), Aristoteles University of Thessaloniki (Greece), Eindhoven University (The Netherlands), INSEAD business school (France), Otto-von-Guericke University (Magdeburg, Germany), and University of Piraeus (Greece). The mission of the group, called RevLog, is to: 1) analyze key issues of reverse logistics, 2) order the issues according to their impact on various industries and society, and 3) build a framework linking these issues.[5]

In the United States, reverse logistics research is supported by the Reverse Logistics Executive Council, an association of practitioners and academics. The headquarters is the Center for Logistics Management, University of Nevada, Reno. Another relevant group is the Reverse Logistics Association, a Fremont, CA-based trade association for third-party service providers who provide reverse logistics services for OEM manufacturers and others.

Research in reverse logistics deals with the following issues:

- What options are there for recovering parts and materials from used products?
- How will the recovery be accomplished?
- Who will do it?
- Can the recovery procedures be carried out within the structure of traditional manufacturing and distribution operations?
- What are the costs and benefits, from both economic and environmental perspectives?

Recovery Methods

Several different types of recovery can be pursued, including the following:

Reuse in present form. In some cases, products can be reused directly, after cleaning and/or some degree of reconstruction. Used pallets and bottles are examples of such products.

Recycled reuse. Some or all of the parts and materials from returned products may be routed to a production or assembly process for making the original product or a different product.

Reuse after repair. A part or material may be repaired, and utilized as a "rebuilt" or "used" product, which may be of lower quality than the original product.

Reuse after remanufacturing. After a product is completely disassembled, its parts and modules are examined and either repaired or replaced. Some upgrading may be performed to make the parts applicable to newer models. Generally, remanufactured products come with warranties comparable to those of totally new products.

Green Programs Add "Green" to the Bottom Line

As time goes by, U.S. companies will have to gear up their commitment to environmental well-being. Even today, they have to comply with environmental regulations in various countries abroad, and soon in most if not all of the EU. In the United States, a number of states have considered various laws and regulations to encourage recycling of used electronics. Currently California, Maryland, and Maine have regulations covering recycling of used computers.

However, mandated compliance is only part of the picture. Recent ongoing research findings demonstrate that companies with the best environmental programs experience significant operating benefits compared to those with the worst or nonexistent programs. Benefits include greater growth in operating income, higher sales-to-assets ratio, greater sales growth, higher earnings-to-assets ratio, higher return on investment, and greater return on assets. The following discussion provides two examples of companies with outstanding environmental programs: Coors Brewing Company in the process industries, and Dell in the electronic manufacturing industries.

Coors Brewing Company's Environmental Programs

In 1959, Coors Brewing Company introduced the aluminum beverage can and aluminum can recycling shortly thereafter. Consumers were willing to participate in can recycling, and the initiative was a success. Throughout the following years, Coors has included environmental responsibility as an ongoing part of its business plan. In March 1990, the company formally adopted the Adolph Coors Company Environmental Principles. The most recent version (called U.S. Environmental, Health & Safety [EHS] Commitment and Policy), adopted in December, 2005 and signed by President and CEO Frits van Paasschen, states in part, "We believe that good business practices embrace environmental stewardship. We are committed to protecting the environment by reducing the environmental impacts of our day-to-day operations at every stage of our product life cycle."[6]

Recycling Programs

Coors follows various major recycling activities to achieve both environmental and bottom-line benefits. The following are a few examples.

Glass. A Coors partner, Rocky Mountain Bottle Company, purchases 79,000 tons of used glass, or cullet, a year. The recycled content of the bottles produced at that company's plant is approximately 30 percent. Recycling glass conserves energy, keeps material out of the landfill, and saves resources. For example, 100 tons of cullet will yield 100 tons of bottles. However, if only virgin materials are used, there is a 15 percent fusion loss. A separate strategy of reducing weights of certain-sized bottles has yielded an annual savings of 72 million pounds of glass.

Packaging. Coors has followed a three-pronged strategy to improve its packaging, by reducing packaging weight, increasing recycled content, and improving recyclability. A redesign of bottle boxes has cut the amount of corrugated Coors uses by 8 million pounds annually. Most of Coors' paper packaging could not be recycled a few years ago. Today, it is 90 percent recyclable.

Two years ago, Coors entered into a nationwide agreement with a waste management firm to improve recycling performance. The partnership has improved the return Coors receives from recycled materials. The partnership team has worked on several projects, including the process for collecting and recycling office waste paper, plastic film, and corrugated. In late 2003, Coors switched its secondary packaging to industry standard claycoat, which is more readily recycled than the metallized film coating used in the past.

Aluminum. Recycling aluminum saves energy and conserves natural resources. The aluminum cans Coors places in the market contain approximately 40 percent recycled content. Recycling aluminum saves 95 percent of the energy needed to produce new metal from raw materials.

Revenue from Byproducts Processing

The following are several examples at Coors of the adage, "Green (in this case recycling) is good business."

Waste beer. Partnering with another company, Coors refines waste beer, a by-product of the brewing process, to produce 1.5 million gallons of ethanol annually. The 200-proof ethanol is blended with gasoline and sold throughout the Rocky Mountain region. A recent expansion has doubled refining capacity to three million gallons a year.

Spent grains are sold as cattle feed, in both wet and dried pellet forms.

Used fermenting yeast is dried and sold to a major pet food manufacturer for use in pet food.

Compost. Not all of the above by-products are suitable for further processing. Some beer that must be destroyed is combined with some spent grains, yeast, and other waste brewing materials to produce compost that is sold in bulk, primarily to commercial landscapers. In addition, damaged wooden pallets previously used in the shipping process are chipped and added to the compost stream.

Reductions in energy use have been realized over a number of years. One of the important reasons for this savings has been a program to sell more wet spent grain. In the past, steam was used to dry the spent grain before selling it for animal feed. By eliminating the drying process, significant energy savings were realized.

Reductions in solid waste (trash) have been achieved, particularly in the case of cardboard. Coors has always recycled cardboard, but a recent baling system has improved the effectiveness of that effort, and substantially cut the amount of cardboard previously sent to landfills.

Bringing Suppliers on Board

A truly effective environmental program must include all members of the supply chain. To this end, Coors works with suppliers to help them improve their environmental performance. For example, Coors presents its Conservation and Environmental Stewardship Grower of the Year Award to an environmentally-conscious barley grower. The top environmental grower is chosen from regional finalists in the Western U.S. states where the company contracts with barley growers. Coors considers the winning growers to be role models for conserving resources and protecting the land.

Bringing Employees on Board

All Coors employees take the company's Workplace Hazard Awareness computer-based training program. Also, employees at the plant level take environmental training more specific to their plant and job function. For example, the Golden, CO brewery requires all employees to go through wastewater minimization training. Training in waste management is also a requirement for many job functions. Awards are presented to the top plants in EHS practices. The award was given to the company's aluminum can manufacturing plant in 2003, the end manufacturing plant in 2004, and the Memphis brewery in 2005. Some of the results achieved at these plants include the following:

- A system was built to incorporate all requirements of a new air-emission permit into plant operating procedures.
- Employees adopted a road next to the plant, and clean it up four times a year.
- The plant is recycling or reusing 96 percent of the solid waste generated at the facility.

- Facility energy consumption has been reduced 13 percent, and water consumption 23 percent over the previous year.
- Employees have sponsored a canoeing river cleanup on the Wolf River, in partnership with the Wolf River conservancy.

The three primary funding principles for Coors' environmental outreach are:

1. There must be a clear business connection to the company.
2. There should be a positive impact to the communities in which Coors has brewing operations (Colorado, Tennessee, and Virginia).
3. There should be an opportunity to build relationships with other organizations, such as environmental groups, regulators, legislators, and other stakeholders.

A Continuing Commitment

As a result of Coors' continuing efforts toward improving the environment, the company has won numerous awards. The following are a few examples:

- U.S. Environmental Protection Agency's Waste Wi$e award for sustained leadership in incorporating waste-prevention actions into its core operations
- EPA Climate Wise Annual Partner Achievement Award for significant accomplishments in improving energy efficiency and reducing pollution
- Coalition of Northeastern Governors' Corporate Commitment Award for leadership in reducing packaging waste
- Circle of Excellence Award from the Distribution Business Management Association.

A commitment to the environment is a formal part of Coors' business strategy. The three key environmental goals of the strategy in 2006 include specific commitments to resource conservation, a targeted reduction in energy consumption and CO_2 emission, and a finalizing of all elements of the company's EHS management system.

In the words of President and CEO van Paasschen, "At Coors, we measure our success not only in terms of our financial performance, but also in terms of our corporate citizenship. How we treat our people, our communities and the environment is very important to us."

Dell's Approach to Green Operations

The electronic products industry has been under scrutiny with regard to how its products and processes may affect the environment. A particular focus has been on disposal of products such as computers when they reach the end of their useful life. One of the leading players in this industry, computer maker Dell, Austin, TX, has committed itself to an environmental policy of managing all stages of a product's total life cycle, from initial concept and design through manufacturing, customer ownership, and end-of-life reuse and recycling.[7]

According to Jake Player, senior manager of Dell's Asset Recovery Services (ARS), the company offers consumers and businesses around the globe a number of ways to "retire" used computers in an environmentally-responsible manner. "We can help business and public institution customers with either value recovery or recycling," he says. "Value recovery includes refurbishment and resale of used computers or parts, with most of the proceeds being returned to the customer." Player notes that for equipment no longer having value, recycling is the usual answer, and to this end Dell helps customers perform environmentally responsible recycling of outdated or non-functional products and parts.

Total Life Cycle Management

Dell believes that each phase of the life of a product, from design to disposal, must be managed with an eye toward eliminating or minimizing impact on the environment. The basic elements of the total life cycle management program are as follows:

Product design. Efficient product recycling and reuse can be factored into the product at the beginning of the design stage. For example, ease of disassembly and recyclability can be designed into the product. The use of hazardous materials can be avoided or minimized by selecting alternative materials, whenever possible, that do not create a disposal problem later on. To this end, Dell has established a Design for the Environment (DfE) program that evaluates and minimizes environmental consequences of actions taken in each phase of the product life cycle, starting with supplier management through to end-of-life reuse or disposal. In addition to material selection, the amount of materials to be used is minimized. Power consumption of the product is another factor considered at this stage.

A new EU directive, RoHS (restriction on the use of hazardous substances), will come into effect this year and will restrict the use of several substances in products sold into the EU. Dell plans to comply with the requirements of the directive globally. It also follows a chemical-use policy that includes a commitment to prohibit the use of all brominated flame retardants in its products. In addition, Dell is in compliance with the EU directive on waste from electrical and electronic equipment (WEEE), which sets criteria for collection, treatment, recycling, and recovery. Dell is also working on compliance with various national laws as they are developed by individual EU member countries to satisfy the directive.

Manufacturing. Dell manufacturing plants have achieved ISO 14001 Environmental Management Systems (EMS) certification (see the section, "Environmental Management System"). As part of this ISO initiative, each location has established goals to improve environmental performance. Improvements are tracked each quarter and progress is reported and discussed at the highest corporate levels. Continuous improvement procedures are followed and shared throughout the company.

Dell makes all products to order. It maintains only three days of inventory for most parts and equipment, thereby minimizing the environmental impact of warehousing. Components and parts are ordered and shipped to Dell on a just-in-time (JIT) basis for final assembly, thus minimizing energy and inventory costs.

The company follows a reduce, reuse, and recycle (R3) policy. All plants have permanent recycling operations that have resulted in major waste reductions. For example, the Dell sites collect more than ten different materials, including cardboard, office paper, plastics, foams, metals, batteries, disks, and pallets. This initiative annually achieves recycling and reuse of about 77,000 tons of material, diverting over 80 percent of non-hazardous solid wastes away from landfills.

Packaging. One goal of Dell's packaging engineers is reducing the amount of overall packaging materials, while still providing the desired level of product protection. Also, Dell tries to improve how it receives materials, and how it ships products to customers. Last year, the company switched to the use of slipsheets instead of pallets for receiving computer chassis and monitors into its facilities. Using slipsheets enables Dell to move more products in each shipping container, so fewer containers need to be used overall. As a result, use of wood has gone down significantly. In the most recent fiscal year, the use of wood was reduced by over 10,000 tons. The company has set a goal of

The Environmental Management System

ISO 14001 is the primary international standard for environmental management systems. Dell's manufacturing facilities and several business functions are ISO 14001 certified. Their environmental management system contains the following components:

- Identifying environmental impacts within manufacturing and other activities
- Setting environmental goals, measuring performance, and reviewing progress
- Establishing procedures for reducing and controlling risks and impacts of its activities, responding to emergencies, and taking corrective action
- Communicating policies and requirements, and training employees, contractors, and others at company sites
- Maintaining records and documentation
- Auditing compliance with regulations and performance of the management system

avoiding the use of 43,000 tons of product packaging and shipping materials between 2003 and 2007. Dell plans to meet this goal through box eliminations, use of slipsheets, and use of alternative materials in its servers, notebooks, and desktops.

Supply chain collaboration. Dell makes most of its components, and many of its products, through partnerships with global suppliers. In so doing, the company requires that suppliers meet its environmental requirements, and also encourages them to integrate environmental management systems into their own operations. In fact, Dell requires its Tier 1 suppliers to be certified in ISO 14001, the primary international standard for environmental management systems, and the OHSAS 18001 program that provides the standard for occupational health and safety management systems.

For the past three years, Dell has held annual environmental webcast "summits" with suppliers. Content of the summits includes the company's supplier code of conduct, product recycling strategies, energy-efficient product designs, and management of restricted materials and chemicals.

Product recovery processes are managed and governed carefully by Dell. The company prohibits its product recovery partners from exporting or landfilling waste from computer recycling projects, and conducts regular audits to ensure that all disposal streams are tracked.

Consumer product reuse or recycling. Dell views its relationships with consumer customers to be a continuum, from acquisition to end-of-life solutions. Various options are available when the primary use of a computer has ended. They are as follows:

- *Donation.* Through Dell's partnership with the National Cristina Foundation, consumers can donate used equipment to charity for a possible tax deduction. The non-profit foundation makes used, functional technology available to disadvantaged children and adults.
- *Recycling.* For outdated or no longer functional computers, Dell provides an environmentally-friendly recycling program in which consumers can participate. The company will accept and pick up any brand of computer, keyboard, mouse, monitor, or printer from the consumer's home, for a $10 fee, or free of charge with the purchase of a new Dell computer. The company will then work with its technology partners to recycle as much of the materials and component parts as is feasible. Another option users may choose to pursue is resale.

Business and institution reuse and recycling. In today's world of growing environmental awareness, dealing with "end-of-life" technology can require as much thought and planning as its initial acquisition and ongoing support (see Figure 3). Dell's ARS unit was developed to make the job easier for business and institutional clients.

Major Steps in Effective Asset Recovery & Recycling

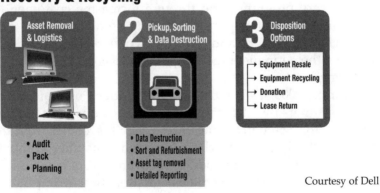

Courtesy of Dell

Figure 3. Dealing with "end-of-life" technology can require as much thought and planning as initial equipment acquisition and support. Especially important is data security, whereby tags and labels are removed, and hard drives overwritten.

According to Jake Player, head of ARS, the services help customers sell, recycle, donate, or complete lease returns of their used computer equipment, including desktop units, notebooks, servers, monitors, printers, batteries, and computer peripherals such as keyboards. The services provide: 1) data security, whereby tags and labels are removed, and hard drives overwritten; 2) cash returns through sale of used equipment); 3) cost savings by eliminating unnecessary storage of used equipment; 4) approved disposal following EPA guidelines; 5) logistics processes to enable recycling or resale activities; 6) single-point accountability; and 7) convenience, allowing customers to focus better on their core businesses.

Training Programs and Ongoing Commitment

Dell employees and full-time contractors are given an introduction to environmental issues when they are hired. Employees working in departments or units that have potential environmental impact also receive training in the ISO 14001 environmental management system. Many are involved in setting environmental goals and working to meet them. Still others are trained in special systems related to their work, such as "Design for EHS" aimed at design and manufacturing engineers. In addition, employees are encouraged to develop local environmental projects.

Overall, the company remains focused on increasing the rate of product recovery, both through providing customers easy and affordable recovery programs, and through increasing customer awareness of the importance of responsibly retiring used computers. At the same time, Dell will continue and improve its own plant recycling programs, including the permanent recycling operations established at each manufacturing location.

During 2005, Dell increased the amount of material recovered from consumers by 72 percent over the previous year, beating a company goal for a 50 percent increase. This effort comes from the following channels: 1) Dell recycling (recycled consumer computer products); 2) ARS (computer products recovered from businesses, governments, schools, and universities); 3) donation (computer products donated to U.S. charities through Dell recycling); and 4) recycling events (computer products dropped off at recycling events sponsored or supported by Dell).

Ray Kulwiec is a writer specializing in material handling, manufacturing, and logistics. Previously he was editor-in-chief of Modern Materials Handling, *senior editor of* Plant Engineering, *and editor-in-chief of* Materials Handling Handbook *(John Wiley & Sons).*

Footnotes

1. Kulwiec, Ray, "Reverse Logistics — The Green Approach," On the Move, Winter 2002, The Material Handling Industry of America, Charlotte, NC.
2. "Logistics networks for the collection and processing of used large white goods," Flapper, S. D. P., H. R. Krikke, and W. S. Vermeulen, Management Report Series 57-1998, 2001, Erasmus University, Rotterdam.
3. Krikke, H. R., "Mandatory recycling of consumer electronics in The Netherlands: a role model for Europe?," Warehouse of the Future 2001, Distribution Business Management Association, Lancaster, PA.
4. http://www.dti.gov.uk/sustainability/weee/index.htm
5. http://www.fbk.eur.nl/OZ/REVLOG/Introduction/Content.htm
6. www.coors.com
7. www.dell.com

Questions

Do your reverse logistics operations include a focus on recycling and reuse of materials?

Do you utilize several different recovery methods?

Are you aware of probable future environmental regulations affecting your company? Are you taking action to deal with them?

Do you seek to have a positive impact on the communities in which you operate? Do you seek to build relationships with environmental groups, regulators, legislators and others?

Section II

Improving Processess

Section 2

Improving
Processes

5

Better Energy Management: Today's Gain, Long-Term Benefits

It's not just about saving some bucks; think about handling supply and price swings, building employee involvement, and eliminating harmful emissions.

Lea A.P. Tonkin

In Brief

Extensive opportunities exist to save energy and money in your facilities. This article describes how a variety of companies, through employee involvement, communication and creative thinking, have achieved meaningful improvements in energy management.

On the next shift break, why not take a moment just to listen? Is that the sound of energy — and money — escaping into thin air? Next, look around in the shop and in the office too. Can you see how inappropriate lighting jacks up your utility bills and may even make your associates' work life more challenging? How about checking the basics of energy outlays for buildings (insulation, etc.), HVAC (heating, ventilation, and air conditioning systems), equipment and machines, motors and vehicles? Are there commonsense ways to reduce your overall energy usage, simply by asking your associates for their ideas? Perhaps the folks at work have been wondering when you'd finally get around to it.

A few questions, as you sort out energy management issues: Do you track energy usage patterns in your operating units? Have you assessed your related supply and financial risks? In turn, how effectively do you use creative, aggregate supply/demand management strategies? Have you upgraded your technology and equipment with energy usage in mind? Are you building energy management expertise within your organization, while culling needed services from outside providers?

Sure, there are folks from the utility companies and plenty of consultants willing to give you their opinions about energy conservation as a means of trimming your operating costs. But you have an opportunity to engage all of your associates in this quest, as an element of your continuous improvement journey. Potential payoffs, besides a lower energy tab, include higher productivity, higher ROI, greater environmental responsibility, and improved overall competitiveness.

DANA Brake Parts Inc. McHenry: People Finding a Better Way

Finding ways to reduce energy usage fits well with the team approach and continuous improvement (CI) philosophy at the DANA Brake Parts Inc. McHenry Facility in McHenry, IL[1]. For example, Martin Moran, plant facilities engineer and environmental/safety coordinator, said energy costs run high for machine shop facilities turning equipment, so it makes good sense to encourage ideas from all employees about frugal energy use (see Figure 1). Rotors, drums, cables, and kit packs for brake repair jobs are manufactured at the plant.

Moran noted that employees have focused on reducing energy usage for some years. Energy conservation and pollution prevention were among the areas documented in the McHenry Facility's ISO

14001 certification, completed in October 1999. Many of the energy-related improvement ideas from associates are common-sense suggestions such as replacing 950 older high-pressure sodium lighting fixtures. The cost savings from this project alone amounts to an estimated $59,000 a year. More efficient

Figure 1: Martin Moran

lighting does not mean a dreary environment. "Replacing old fixtures and painting the ceilings white makes it brighter and nicer for employees, while we save energy and cost," said Moran.

"We used to leave equipment running between shifts and on weekends due to start-up problems. Now, with appropriate equipment modifications, we shut it off, to reduce our energy use. We also replaced or rebuilt some old CNC (computer numerically-controlled) equipment," Moran continued. "Our voluntary energy and recycling committees also help with this effort and other improvements. For example, our energy committee worked on replacing compressors with new high-efficiency compressors with a heat recovery system. The heat recovery system will allow us to use the 'waste heat' in the winter to reduce energy use. Four dust collection systems (35,000 cfm each) pull air and dust off machines to a dust collector outside the building. Depending on the season, the filtered air is routed in or out of the building; this system helps to relieve the load and lowers natural gas usage. We are considering replacing all of our fluorescent lighting with high-efficiency fixtures, ballasts, and T-8 bulbs. We are reducing air leaks on our system with a CI program. We have also replaced two of our large air conditioning units with high-efficiency units."

Kaizen projects and efforts to glean improvement ideas from employees result in many smaller, day-by-day changes which lead to better energy management at DANA Brake Parts Inc. McHenry. "We have an Idea Program — People Finding a Better Way — to encourage every employee to come up with two improvement ideas each month (see the company's suggestion form in Figure 2)," Moran said. "These are often ideas that employees can implement themselves." Employees receive "DANA Dollars" for their implemented improvement ideas, which can be exchanged for gift certificates redeemable at local stores.

Corporate Support for Plant-Level Improvements: 3M

Making it easier for employees to use energy wisely and to develop energy projects is a continuing priority at 3M. The company provides internal website information about best practices in energy management, as well as related metrics, and energy management project data. "We look at energy use as an important part of overall operating costs and effectiveness," said Steve Schultz, energy program manager at 3M, St. Paul, MN.

DANA *People Finding A Better Way* -Through Ideas

36496

Date _____ Clock# _____

Name _____ _____

Coach Approval / Date   Yes _____ / _____ No _____

Implemented / Date   Yes _____ / _____ No _____

Helper _____

My Idea Is: _____

_____

_____

_____

_____

White: Office   Yellow: File Copy   Pink: Employee

Figure 2: DANA's suggestion form

"Our corporation has a goal of improving energy effectiveness by four percent each year," Schultz said. "That translates into specific goals for each facility. We have an energy champion and an energy team at each facility to develop and implement projects." A closely-watched metric is energy used per unit of product. Internal and external benchmarking projects, annual energy management conference, communications support such as posters, articles in employee publications, and an employee intranet website encourage these efforts.

Schultz noted successful projects at 3M's Menomonie, WI plant as examples of the organization's broad approach to energy management. Approximately 450 employees at the facility manufacture tapes, optical films, reflective sheeting, ceramic fibers, and other products, handling production for 12 3M divisions.

The plant initially worked on improving the efficiency of lighting systems, utilizing the U.S. EPA's Energy Star Program. This effort resulted in an annual savings of $69,325. Following this success, the plant formed a cross-functional (engineering, plant engineering, and production) energy team and selected an energy champion for the plant. Team members worked with an engineering consulting firm to identify and implement other energy-saving projects.

The energy team used 3M's Energy Implementation Guide (which provides step-by-step suggestions for improving energy efficiency).

The team's strategies included:

- Implement effective energy management programs
- Promote energy conservation awareness
- Encourage continuous energy conservation improvements

3M's Menomonie, WI Projects

A steam to hot water heat exchanger was among the team's projects. The plant installed steam boilers for heating systems (steam and glycol); a heat exchanger for the system (used for heating sinks and bathrooms) enabled the facility to shut down an older, less efficient hot water boiler.

Turning off PCs and stand-alone printers at night and during the weekends also could decrease energy use, the team determined. They worked with the information technology (IT) department on their plan for cycling the devices. They checked model numbers for all the devices, compared them to energy-saving charts, and calculated potential savings. The team sent email messages to individuals about turning off their PCs and printers, with reminder emails every four months. A walk-through by the plant energy team champion showed 75 percent participation. After discussion with the remaining 25 percent, participation reached 90 percent.

A process engineer, a division engineer, a maintenance technician, a production supervisor, and an operator at Menomonie conducted a production process study in an area where equipment had been intentionally oversized for process flexibility during start-up and development. The under-utilized equipment (two 30-hp blowers) was replaced by smaller, more efficient components (two 10-hp blowers with variable frequency drives); the older equipment was moved to support other areas of the process. A 100-hp air compressor and a 30-hp exhaust blower as well as a dryer were removed; installation of more efficient equipment and a dryer modification enabled the changes.

After monitoring operation of a plastic film production extruder, the energy team recommended adding an extruder barren insulating jacket (it cost $1,394). They had calculated potential payback in six months from energy savings. Actual results indicated that the barrel blankets reduced electrical energy needed to maintain extruder temperatures by 45 percent. A bonus: excess heat was eliminated, cutting air conditioning requirements and related cost.

The Menomonie energy team and other employees' innovative ways resulted in even more savings. For example, they modified the air handler control strategy (serving production and office areas); an occupied/unoccupied schedule allowed modifications in usage of fans and heating/cooling coils; static pressure set point adjustments and humidifier steam usage modifications were made. Further savings resulted from installation of an air-cooled chiller to replace plant-generated chilled water. The list goes on.

Thanks to these efforts, the plant saved $159,168 a year in electrical costs and 44 million BTUs. The local electric utility recognized the plant for conserving enough energy to power 600 homes for one year. Additional information about 3M's environment/energy activities is available at its website (http://www.3m.com.)

Brown Printing: Energy Audit, Efficient Pollution Control Equipment

Sometimes the simplest energy conservation solutions work best according to John Kruse, technical director at Brown Printing Company, Woodstock, IL, owned by Bertelsmann AG. Turning to the University of Illinois at Chicago Industrial Assessment Center (UIC IAC) for energy audit assistance, for example, netted several basic improvement suggestions that cut energy use and boosted overall productivity, Kruse said.[2] Among the student auditors' suggestions: Make sure air conditioning equipment is cleaned at the start of the season; replace older compressors to eliminate emissions while equipment is off; turn off unused lighting and equipment.

"Talk to equipment suppliers and involve all employees in your energy conservation activities," suggested Kruse. He noted that teamwork with supplier Eisenmann Corporation in Crystal Lake, IL on the purchase of an Eisenmann valveless regenerative thermal oxidizer (VRTO) equipment buy helped to reduce emissions and decrease energy use. VRTOs destroy volatile organic compounds (VOCs) that can contribute to higher ozone levels. VOCs are typically emitted as the ink dries on a page in a dryer. As the Eisenmann CRTO oxidizes VOCs into harmless compounds, it recovers heat from the process exhaust, eliminating the need for additional heat or energy.

Open Kitchens: Think Beyond Initial Cost

Rick Fiore, president and owner of contract food service company Open Kitchens, Chicago, also noted the power of energy audits. He and Mike Hartwig, refrigeration manager, worked with consultant John Katrakis (see the box, "Power Plays: Develop Effective Strategies") to trim energy bills. Hartwig said that an energy audit showed the need for more efficient lighting and other changes (lighting costs decreased 50 percent after energy-saver ballasts were installed in place of older ballasts).[3]

Buying oversized condensers on refrigeration units, buying more efficient compressors for freezers, and installing a new, white Bond Cote roof ("expensive, but it will pay for itself because we won't have as much trouble cooling offices," said Fiore) also lowered energy bills.[4] "You've got to think beyond the initial cost," said Hartwig.

Lockheed Martin: Buy Smart, Use Less Energy

Energy conservation activities at Lockheed Martin complement overall corporate performance improvement programs, according to Bob McMullen, director of corporate energy management for the company's Corporate Energy, Environment, Safety, & Health (EESH) unit. "We're on a simple strategy: Buy smart, use less," he said. "Cost is the principal factor, and we also benefit the environment by reducing greenhouse gas emissions." McMullen believes in building internal expertise while making effective use of external energy procurement strategy specialists (see the box, "Power Plays: Develop Effective Strategies").

On the supply side, said McMullen, Lockheed Martin was purchasing natural gas through approximately 20 to 25 agreements negotiated independently by each facility. "Now we are buying through Summit, using a common process for these agreements, but still buying at various times and for varying durations. Next we want to buy all of our requirements in common corporate purchase and allocate gas to facilities based on usage requirements, enabling us to manage price risk more effectively," he said.

The other side of the equation is demand, or load. McMullen noted that corporate programs support significant energy use reduction programs at the facility level. "We track energy use (or consumption) and cost by business unit and by facility," McMullen said. "Our business units take responsibility for efficiency improvements and usage reductions. It might mean turning out lights in hallways, setting thermostats higher in the summertime, shutting off equipment during peak usage periods, etc. We provide support with capital funds earmarked exclusively for energy efficiency projects, and encouragement

Power Plays: Develop Effective Strategies

Looking for additional expertise in your energy buys and overall energy management? You can call on a wide range of consultants — independents, some affiliated with large consulting groups or utilities, etc. Here are tips from two consultants:

Understand Your Organization's Needs and Watch Out for the Landmines

Outsourcing energy management functions makes sense for industrial and commercial organizations, according to Phil Wafford, vice president of Summit Energy, Louisville, KY, and energy procurement strategist working with industrial and commercial end users. Overall energy management strategy assistance can be provided, as well as tactical management, Wafford said. Among specific services: reviewing bills and reconciling them for audits, evaluating rates and considering alternative energy sourcing strategies, developing budget plans, and developing long-term strategies, etc.

"Yesterday's world is different from today's world," Wafford said. "End users, for example, need to be proactive and consider change to survive in today's deregulated environment. There are more opportunities, as well as risks. Landmines come in all forms in both a regulated and deregulated natural gas and electric power energy market. For example, it may make sense to lock in a percentage of your energy supply for a period of time, based on the risk tolerance that your company is willing to take. However, a mistake can be made by trying to streamline energy buys with one supplier. If that supplier ends up filing bankruptcy, what happens to the position you had? Facility managers need to develop and understand their risk tolerance levels.

"There is no single strategy that answers all needs." Wafford continued. "It is important to understand what is important to your organization — preventing liability, saving dollars, building widgets? Then, define the components that can go into driving total cost and what you can do relative to each component and associated risks. Summit can help make these recommendations, to be consistent with what senior management is trying to define in their corporate energy goals."

Energy Efficiency Surveys, Process Improvements

The transition from regulated monopolies to open access markets and real-time pricing is stimulating businesses to take advantage of lower-priced energy. Regional differences in pricing, availability, and regulatory environments are among the factors affecting industrial and commercial energy purchases, noted John Katrakis of J.T. Katrakis & Associates, Barrington, IL, energy and environmental management consultants. "Rolling blackouts may affect companies in one region on a seasonal basis, and not be a concern in other areas," he said. Political unrest, wars, etc. also impact energy pricing and availability in global markets. "The Middle East war jitters are the cause of the recent dramatic spike in the cost of natural gas," said Katrakis.

The size of the utility bill also has a large influence on the energy purchase opportunities available to an organization. "Large industries have been able to shop around for energy longer than smaller companies and to this day can negotiate terms and take advantage of opportunities not available to the smaller businesses," according to Katrakis.

"Given all of the uncertainties in energy markets, there are many good reasons for reducing your company's overall energy consumption," he said. "Reducing energy use guarantees protection against future sharp swings in energy prices," he added. Reduced energy loads also make it easier to install back-up energy sources to deal with lapses in the reliability of energy supplies.

Energy-saving improvements may also bring other benefits. "For example, energy efficiency surveys not only can help management find ways to decrease energy cost. They can help improve environmental performance, and increase productivity; energy-saving process changes may enable higher output per hour, in some cases," said Katrakis.

"When you're conducting an energy survey, start with lighting, heating, ventilation, and air conditioning systems," the consultant continued. Significant reductions in electric and gas requirements often result from such surveys. Lighting system changes may offer a payback period of one or two years. Newer lighting systems can improve task and overall lighting for employees — another bonus. "Don't forget the building 'envelope' or structure; you may find opportunities here to reduce ventilation loads as well as heating and cooling loads," he said.

Even more energy savings can be gained by looking at specific processes, the various plating and anodizing baths used by metal finishers, the drying processes and pollution control processes used in printing companies, etc.

"Make sure you and your energy consultant work with your equipment vendor on any process improvements," Katrakis said. "Your equipment vendor will help ensure that any changes will not have an adverse impact on productions...vendors may suggest modifications and provide consulting assistance that will not only reduce your utility costs — it may also increase the productivity of your staff. For example, in printing businesses, improving the control of the ink drying process reduces spoiled products as well as energy costs. Eliminating leaks and improving the control of compressed air systems, used to convey paper and cuttings, reduces downtime due to paper jams and reduces energy costs...The improvements in productivity resulting from energy-focused interventions can end up being more valuable than the avoided energy costs."

with awareness programs, banners, and other communications." A corporate intranet website provides information on environmental and conservation "best practices" and project information.

Challenges include sorting through technical aspects of promising alternative processes, creating additional employee awareness (some facilities such as in Sunnyvale, CA have dealt with rolling blackouts, while availability may not seem as great a concern in other areas), benchmarking, etc. "Where there is a combination of office and warehouse assembly and research operations, it's difficult to find what our level of world-class performance should be," said McMullen. He noted that the E SOURCE organization's website (see the reference list) offers energy management best practice information.

Energy Management at Lockheed Martin, Orlando, FL: "Fairly High Level of Maturity"

With a site population of over 4,000 employees, and facilities covering approximately 2.1 million sq. ft. (1 million sq. ft. offices, 800,000 sq. ft. factory and lab space, and the rest, warehouse and distribution), energy management specialists are always on the lookout for innovative strategies at Lockheed Martin Missiles and Fire Control operation in Orlando, FL. Energy management here has reached "a fairly high level of maturity," according to Don Wilson, technical services manager-facilities at Orlando. "We started with the low-hanging fruit, moved on to technical and operation concerns; and now we coordinate with Environments, Safety, and Health (ESH) activities," he said. "I deal mostly in encouraging awareness."

All Lockheed Martin employees have access from the corporation about activities that can work well at work or at home. "ISO 14001 information is online; goals we have worked at one time or another as ISO goals include energy conservation; safety and health; recycling; and water conservation," said Sorina Terrell, environmental engineer.

Performance Management Teams (PMTs — process for natural work groups to form teams) are accountable for tracking and improving performance on selected metrics, added Terrell. Overall performance gains reflect progress in reducing all forms of waste, including energy use. An energy management contractor also reviews site utility bills each month. PMTs gain management's support and "ear" through regular reporting of their results.

"Every team in Production Operations meets weekly to review their metric performance as they strive for continuous improvement. They generate productivity items to improve quality, reduce cost to the customer, and generate savings for the benefit of the company. This is a process that works and our trends continue to improve year after year because the teams make it happen," said Victoria Myers-Holder, a PMT manager at the Lockheed Martin Orlando site. "We process and implement over 1,000 ideas annually ranging from energy conservation and limited use of chemicals to quality, cost and schedule improvements."

Dealing with Energy Hogs in All Areas

Don't confine energy-monitoring to production and research areas, advised Terrell and Wilson. "We've found a surprising amount of payback from energy conservation efforts — better lighting management in conference rooms, for example. They're notorious energy-wasters," he said. Installing motion sensors that turn off lights in unused conference rooms, offices and bathrooms led to a one-year payback in some cases.

"Great savings from lighting controls also resulted from the Orlando operations' timed schedule," Wilson said. Lights are automatically turned off 30 to 40 minutes after a shift. After-hours timers pulse the lights off at intervals, in case someone wanders through an area after the shift is over and turns on the lights; workers can turn on the lights for extended, late or weekend work periods.

"Energy Star-related PCs have a sleep feature," Wilson continued. "That feature saves us $50,000 to $60,000 a year. Otherwise, those PCs would be sitting there and churning watts — energy hogs, sucking power 24 hours a day."

Lessons Learned at Lockheed Martin Missiles and Fire Control—Orlando

Energy management "lessons learned" offered by Wilson and Terrell included:
- Communicate continuously and through several means such as meetings, posters, training sessions, an internal website, "Turn It Off" and "Think Green" stickers and table toppers, employee updates on work area monitors, etc.

- Mindset changes and awareness rather than enforced improvements should be emphasized, as you monitor performance.
- Set realistic goals, and put a price tag on progress — for example, a new boiler may pay for itself in two years as a result of related energy savings.
- Keep senior management up to date on energy management efforts.
- Maintain a long-term improvement perspective as you look for day-to-day progress.

Wilson noted that Lockheed Martin has a certain amount of funding available from corporate solely for energy conservation activities. "This way, we don't compete at the site level for improvement project funds," he said.

Lockheed Martin's Sunnyvale, CA Operations: "Make Changes Part of Everyday Life"

While rolling blackouts and heat alerts catch headlines and employee attention, long-term progress in meeting sustainability goals is a key issue, said Rich Robertson, manager Bay Area technical maintenance service, Lockheed Martin Missiles and Space, Sunnyvale, CA. Robertson said that, after focusing on energy conservation for a number of years, associates at Sunnyvale must work creatively to continue reducing power requirements. Energy usage at the site dropped five percent in 2002 in addition to the 13 percent reduction from the previous year.

"We have been working on behavioral changes, after working with a consultant," Robertson continued. "You can't start energy management programs and just walk away from them. You need to constantly look for ways to make these changes part of everyday life with the focus on minimizing waste and containing costs."

An Energy Conservation Management Plan for all operating divisions developed in partnership with Robertson's group covers long-term energy savings ideas; rapid response energy usage reductions and related contacts; black-out risk mitigation suggestions; implementation and maintenance; primary contacts by building; and related topics. The rapid response reduction topics include a rapid shutdown plan for non-essential equipment and lighting as well as details of a plan

Energy Management References

- http://www.newsdata.com/enernet/conweb Pacific Northwest Energy Conservation & Renewable Energy Newsletter; full version at Con.WEB
- http://www.ase.org/e-FFICIENCY Alliance to Save Energy's e-FFICIENCY NEWS monthly newsletter
- http://www.energyideas.org EnergyIdeas Clearinghouse managed by Washington State University Cooperative Extension Energy Program; see also ConWEB above
- www.eweb.org Energy Web
- http://www.esource.com E SOURCE — provides renewable power, etc. information for energy service providers, major energy users and others
- http://www.gri.org GTI (Gas Technology Institute) — research, development, and training organization; information on efficient burner systems, gasification technology, etc.
- www.naem.org National Association for Environmental Management — environments, energy, etc. information and related events.
- www.ouc.com Orlando Utilities Commission
- http://www.svmg.org Silicon Valley Manufacturing Group — this organization works with government officials on issues ranging from reliable energy and sustainable environment to quality education, etc.
- www.steamingahead.org and also www.steamingahead.ase.org The Steaming Ahead newsletter features tips for improving steam systems and is a gateway to steam efficiency resources.
- http://www.eren.doe.gov and also http://www.eere.energy.gov U.S. Department of Energy including Energy Efficiency and Renewable Energy gateway to websites and documents.
- www.epa.gov U.S. Environmental Protection Agency

The assistance of Sorina Terrell from Lockheed Martin Missiles and Fire Control operations in Orlando, FL in compiling this reference list is appreciated.

identifying contacts, where, and how these actions will take place. Among the black-out risk mitigation topics are shifts starting earlier to ensure that anodizing and baking of adhesive primers are completed by noon; backup generators to be used where possible for autoclaves and ovens during power loss; and earlier work shifts to prevent damage to high-value hardware. Implementation and maintenance areas covered in the guidelines range from building energy managers established for all responsible facilities to formal energy awareness sessions, weekly self-audits, visual power reduction reminders, and ice cream celebrations for 100 percent success on audits.

Site work groups and specialized maintenance, etc. teams target specific energy usage reduction goals. They also gain pointers from company website project data and trade energy-saving ideas with fellow members of the Silicon Valley Manufacturing Group (see the accompanying reference list). Employees receive feedback on energy usage numbers related to the site's overhead costs and budget through a company website. Consistent communications (posters, meetings, internal news articles, etc.) with associates encourage awareness of energy and environmental issues.

Slashing Energy Waste and Costs

Robertson said the Sunnyvale associates' successful campaign to reduce electricity and gas usage in 2001 reflected improvements on many fronts. After learning that electricity costs were projected to jump 84 percent for the five million sq. ft. of operations in the Bay area compared to 2000 costs, they launched a Demand Reduction Program, plant operating efficiencies — lighting retrofits, and an employee energy conservation awareness program.

Robertson said the site's energy team reviewed utility bills, historical data from a computer monitoring program and building meters, air handler time schedules, amperage readings on centrifugal chillers and selected buildings, automated lighting systems performance, manufacturing/test equipment use and work schedules, and other factors. They also audited non-automated lighting systems and computer monitors.

Next, Robertson led an energy team in the planning and development project phase. The team included an energy coordinator, an HVAC supervisor and analyst, an energy management systems (EMS) manager, and two industrial electronic technicians. Their audits showed that HVAC systems consumed the most energy, followed by lighting, production equipment, and office equipment.

The energy team then developed a project list targeting the largest energy users, bearing in mind the required investment and projected payback. An allocation of $1.2 million in capital funds from Lockheed Martin accounting enabled the technical maintenance department to use $500,000 from deferred maintenance projects for energy management. The energy team also partnered with the site's long-term lighting service company on delamping and lighting upgrade projects. The Sunnyvale energy team looked to the electric utility firm for cost reductions based on power usage decreases during peak periods; upgrades in lighting, air conditioning, and refrigeration; and other conservation measures.

Efficiency measures ranged from upgrading lighting and delamping to use of energy-efficient replacement motors, automating a 9000-ton capacity chiller complex, HVAC operation reviews and other process changes, replacement of weather stripping on exit doors, and increased frequency of preventative maintenance on the site's energy management systems (plus employee awareness programs).

Conservation activities, meanwhile, included changing thermostats from 75 degrees to 78 degrees F for cooling, and lowering the heating settings two degrees to 68 degrees F, for a savings of $2 million annually. Many other steps also lowered the energy tab: resetting HVAC time schedules, delamping parking lots to city standards, calibrating motion sensors, and switching janitors' schedules to day shift only to reduce the use of lighting at night. Manufacturing groups changed start times from 6 a.m. to 5 a.m. (in some cases 4 a.m.). Moving startup times for Test Services equipment such as large vacuum pumps also reduced peak period energy costs.

Gas consumption costs were reduced through the use of negotiations on utility contracts and shutting off the hot water heating boiler systems when not needed. In some HVAC systems, design may prevent that action, but carefully thought-out control strategies can compensate in milder climates. For example, in multi-zone systems, raising the cold deck supply air to 60 degrees and starting the air handlers one to two hours later can compensate for boilers turned off. This approach resulted in a 20 percent energy usage reduction.

Employee outreach and education programs helped to generate awareness and better energy management practices. The executive vice president assigned each vice president a group or chunk of buildings ("Chunker"); the vice presidents were responsible for developing an energy team and conservation plan for the Chunkers.

Thanks to these combined efforts, Lockheed Martin Missiles and Space energy management programs (Sunnyvale and Palo Also, CA operations) improved energy reliability, brought $4.8 million in cost avoidance/financial savings annually; cut energy use by 15 megawatts daily, decreased electricity use 13.6 percent, and trimmed natural gas usage 17.3 percent in 2001. The conservation efforts continue.

Energy management suggestions from Robertson:
- Senior management involvement at the corporate and site level is critical for maintaining the conservation focus.
- Study energy usage during peak demand periods (noon to 6 p.m.) and evaluate possible shifts in some processes to earlier start times or consolidating processes.
- Look for creative ways to bring home the message of wise energy use; an energy fair (featuring educational displays and giveaway coffee cups, mouse pads, etc.) drew 2,500 of the Sunnyvale site's 8,000 employees. Employees contributed energy-saving ideas in a "Dining in the Dark" contest to win a candelabra. Newsletters, stickers, the company website, posters, employee meetings, etc. also build conservation awareness.
- More meters mean better building-by-building breakdowns on energy usage.
- Monitor energy usage at night or after the regular shifts end.
- Use out-of-the-box thinking on shutting off equipment you may not need.
- Plan for regular HVAC maintenance and lighting upgrades in renovations, as you make energy management plans.

"You need a siege mentality, to take out the waste — including energy usage — in all processes," said Robertson. "Find ways to break down energy use by work areas or types of usage, and then ask employees for their ideas. Many of their ideas are 'free,' fresh and applicable.

"At our sites, many employees participated, and according to our audits, continue to keep the good habits," added Robertson. "Automation of systems certainly helps. That doesn't mean we can relax. We want to continue to do our part in supporting operating efficiencies and pollution preventions, all of which reduces overall operating costs."

Lea A.P. Tonkin, Woodstock, IL is the editor of Target *magazine.*

Notes

1 The Brake Parts Inc. facility in Crystal Lake, IL was among the plant tour sites for AME's Annual Conference during November, 2002.

2 The UIC IAC is part of a nationwide program sponsored at more than 20 universities by the U.S. Department of Energy (check the website http//www.erc.uic.edu and

look for the IAC information at the site). It is designed to help small and midsized companies. Check the website oit.doe.gov for more information. Mike Chimack of UIC IAC said energy use audits frequently uncover waste in lighting systems, compressed air usage, and waste streams; single-pass cooling systems used in metal casting work are common culprits too.

3 Open Kitchens' lighting supplier for the newer bulbs was All Tech Lighting, Schaumburg, IL.

4 The BondCote material, made by Bond Cote Corporation in Pulaski, VA was obtained through Century Roofing Corporation, Calumet Park, IL.

Questions

Are all employees of your organization involved in managing energy use? Do you have improvement initiatives focused on energy use?

Do you share information internally about best practices in energy use?

Does your company have specific goals for improving energy effectiveness?

Has your company had an energy audit?

6

The Future of Energy in Manufacturing

A ration examination of energy sources for manufacturing in the 21st century: Part 1 of 2 parts.

Dr. John R. Wilson

In Brief

We are not about to run out of fossil fuel energy, but for various reasons our energy future is not bright. Expect energy to become much more costly, and that environmental issues will be impossible to neglect. Wilson explains why in Part 1 of a two-part series.

Sometimes it seems that more trash is talked about our energy future than on the basketball court. People who really understand the science and engineering of energy, or who have a sound appreciation of what can and cannot be done with "new" fuels seldom enter the public forum. Instead, we have been treated with endless books and magazine articles from writers like Amory Lovins and Jeremy Rifkin. In general, these writers appear to reach their conclusions without a comprehensive foundation in technical and economic fact.

Those of us who make energy choices for industrial applications or forecast the real future of energy have a serious responsibility first to assimilate all the facts we can. Switching fuels on a large scale has a big economic impact. Not only is the cost of changeover high, the ongoing cost of alternate fuels must be projected with more quantitative certainty than out-of-thin-air numbers in the popular press. Guesswork is not good enough.

Outline

In Part 1 of this series, we will review the sources and future availability of conventional fossil fuels. Fossil fuels are finite in total quantity and will obviously decline in supply at some point in the future, but contrary to claims, we are not "running out of fossil energy." (Readers motivated primarily by environmental concerns may wish that we were, be we aren't — at least not yet.) We can roughly project the future availability of fuels in use today, and their future cost. We're going to pay much more for them, but we're not running out.

The real issues facing (or not facing) conventional fuels such as crude oil and natural gas may surprise you. We certainly expect changes, but maybe not those broadly publicized. Global warming is an important issue, if a tangled one. It will affect our energy choices, but won't eliminate them. Along the way, we will look at ways to increase or extend the supply of conventional fuels such as oil and natural gas.

Part 2, in a following issue of *Target*, will review the advantages and disadvantages of alternative fuels that are often claimed to be available (and sometimes better) than those in common use today. The list includes hydrogen, biodiesel, and other possible biofuels (such as ethanol, biomass, and some synthetic diesel fuels) as well as the future role of coal as a source for synthetic natural gas and many other energy products.

Global Warming (GW)

Discussion of global warming can become quite muddled, but a couple of things about it are quite clear to all parties closely involved:
  a) Global warming is real — it is happening and its consequences are a curious mix of good news and bad news, except to those who think that any change is bad.
  b) Carbon dioxide is at least partly responsible for global warming, but its direct contribution may be quite small.
Beyond these two broadly agreed statements, everything that has been written should be considered highly speculative. For example, CO_2 is not the only contributor to global warming. In fact, it may not be the largest direct contributor. Water vapor, a GW agent about as effective as CO_2, probably plays that role. Most water vapor is the result of evaporation from global surface warming. Other non-CO_2 factors

include the steady increase in solar radiation that has been a factor in GW since about 1850!

What we do not know with any certainty, given the huge lack of precision of the models used to predict GW and the uncertainty of the assumptions that they include, is whether a reduction in atmospheric CO_2 will result in any benefits at all. Until we achieve greater certainty predicting the influence of CO_2, it seems highly inappropriate to invest the amount of money called for by the Kyoto Treaty in CO_2 reduction activity.

There seems to be no doubt that CO_2 is being absorbed in large quantities by the oceans. The resulting decrease in pH (increase in acidity) may be having a negative effect on marine life. This requires much more investigation.

Given all the uncertainties, it's probably better to limit CO_2 emissions than not — despite some of the effects of global warming being desirable! Although the "computer modelists" and the very noisy Union of Concerned Scientists are cocksure of it, we really do NOT know whether cutting CO_2 emissions, or even reducing the total atmospheric CO_2 levels, will achieve any improvement in either global warming or marine acidity. Hopefully, this thinking is behind the intent of the present U.S. Administration to call for more facts before imposing on industry the huge expense required to reduce CO_2 production below present levels.

The low-hanging fruit has already been picked; there are no more easy solutions to CO_2 reduction. However, several companies in the oil industry report surprising themselves by finding that changes to reduce CO_2 emissions also resulted in fuel savings. That's the non-obvious side of something obvious to remember. Greater efficiency using energy also reduces CO_2 emissions.

Crude Oil

Without doubt, world-wide, we have a fixed amount of crude oil in the ground. That amount is no longer increasing — notwithstanding some ingenious but unsupported theories about continuous natural production somewhere deep in the earth. Because of that, of course we are running out of oil on a global scale, but globally we will not exhaust the earth's supply any time soon. However, in some locations, national proven reserves are running short. The United States is one of those locations; production has been declining for many years. When you don't have it, you have to import it, often in large annual quantities. So we are running out of oil, but only locally, regionally, or nationally — not globally. Of course, countries that depend on imported oil (the UK, the United States, Japan, Korea, for example), are concerned about any interruption of supplies, and also about the ability of OPEC and other overseas sources (such as Russia and Libya) to raise the international price of oil by controlling the supply.

The Hubbert Peak

Because of the depletion of oil reserves in some major producing regions, their rate of production has declined. In any region, a plot of oil production in, say, barrels/year against the year of production reaches a peak — a year in which production is at maximum — after which it declines. The maximum is referred to as the "Hubbert Peak." The year of this peak obviously varies widely from oilfield to oilfield, region to region, country to country. It also depends on many "man-made" factors such as the aggressiveness of the exploration and pro-duction practices and especially on whether advanced secondary and tertiary recover techniques are widely used.

Many oilfields, especially in the United States, are well past their Hubbert Peak, with production in decline. In fact, the United States as a whole, well past its Hubbert Peak (1970), is now importing about 60 percent of its oil. However, other countries and regions are far from reaching their Hubbert Peaks, based on proven reserves alone, and ignoring large amounts of incompletely documented oil in the ground. (Much of the argument is about the quality of reserve calculations.) An additional complication is that the usual Hubbert Peak calculation ignores vast amounts of unconventional oil in deposits like the Canadian Oil Sands in Alberta, the Orinoco Belt heavy oil deposits in Venezuela, and the vast, but difficult-to-recover shale oil deposits found mainly in Utah and Colorado.

Most Hubbert Peak projections, developed by environmentalists who are keen to see the "end of oil," also ignore vast amounts of oil in place in older, depleted reservoirs. This is oil that was not recovered earlier, but that can now be recovered — at higher cost — by advanced secondary and tertiary recovery techniques. But the cost of recovering oil, sands oil, shale oil, and deep offshore oil is a lot more expensive than that. To make these recovery operations profitable, crude prices must rise far higher than historical norms. As this article is written, the price of low-sulfur premium crude is about U.S. $48/barrel (42 U.S. gallons or about 294 lb. per barrel), high enough to sustain oil sands production but far from enough to support shale oil recovery (which requires at least $60–70/bbl).

Thus, we are approaching or have already passed the Hubbert Peak for conventional oil, or "Cheap Oil" (as the June 2004 National Geographic Magazine pointed out), but we are by no means running out of oil, despite what oil-haters would like you to believe. On the contrary, globally we have ample oil supplies for many years, but its price will undoubtedly rise both because of demand and its high cost of recovery. Near term, in a free market (which OPEC may not permit!) we expect the price to decline perhaps to U.S. $35–40/bbl this year; then begin to rise again — and continue to rise.

Also, oil is currently priced in U.S. dollars. Valued against international currencies such as the Euro, the dollar has been in free fall the past two years. Oil producers world-wide have thus seen a decline in buying power of their receipts of about 35 percent or at least $10/bbl. While this decline has been offset by the run-up in prices, it also serves to put a floor under the price of oil. We are unlikely ever again to see high-grade (low sulfur or "sweet") crude oil at less than $35/bbl.

But perhaps the most critical factor in the price of crude oil is its quality. This is measured by its sulfur content, by its API gravity ("light" is better), or its volatiles content (such as environmentally unfriendly aromatic hydrocarbons). Quality varies widely around the globe and even within most of the major oil-producing countries. Because of the emphasis over the past two or three decades on controlling sulfur emission, "clean" low-sulfur crudes have been in great demand. These premium crude oils have therefore been depleted much faster than heavier, high-sulfur crudes. As a result, the world is running out of "good stuff" at a time when demand for low-sulfur crude is increasing, for example to make ultra-low sulfur diesel fuel (ULSD).

Plenty of technology is available for processing heavier, higher-sulfur crude. Most of it involves hydrogenation and catalytic processing, which incurs additional capital costs and additional operating costs. Sulfur-free distillate products such as ULSD are more costly when made from heavier crudes containing more sulfur. We have a severe lack of facilities capable of handling them, especially in the United States. Consequently, the prices of high-sulfur crudes are much lower than the prices of low-sulfur light crudes. In fact high-sulfur crudes currently glut the market in those countries having too much of them, like Saudi Arabia, Iraq, and Canada.

Recovering these heavy crudes requires an additional step, crude upgrading, which has become quite common in Canada and in Venezuela. Upgraded crude is then indistinguishable from conventional crude. Obviously, when the price differential between high-sulfur and low-sulfur crudes reaches the right point, upgrading will become more prevalent elsewhere — investments will be made.

Impact on Manufacturing

Although we will not run out, crude oil and its derivatives such as diesel fuel, jet fuel and gasoline will become progressively more expensive over the next several decades. As prices increase, manufacturers may want to consider switching to alternative energy sources. The question is: "to what"?

If a manufacturer must raise steam or generate electricity on site, choices seem to be narrowing. Thanks in part to switching to natural gas for power generation from 1970–1990, we are truly running out of conventional natural gas. U.S. natural gas proven reserves amount to little more than a ten-year supply, but much more is available internationally. Although coal reserves are ample, both in the United States and world-wide, it is unlikely that anyone would find acceptable a major switch back to directly burning coal in manufacturing plants' power stations. The electric power industry and its regulators continue to use outdated coal technology, ignoring newer "clean coal" technology, which has received little publicity, but has promise.

Natural Gas

The United States uses 23 trillion cubic feet of natural gas annually, not only producing at maximum rates from all domestic fields, but importing gas from Canada (whose reserves are also limited). It's beginning to import large amounts of liquefied natural gas (LNG) from Trinidad and (in the future) elsewhere. Recent discoveries have been minimal, partly because the price of natural gas was only about $2.50/MCF for a long time. It now averages about $6.50 (having shot much higher in 2004). That level is stimulating much additional exploration, but not much additional discovery. The price is likely to remain high.

It is imperative that the United States and Canada find additional natural gas. Plenty of gas is known to exist in difficult-to-reach deposits — for example, deep offshore in the Gulf of Mexico, in what are called "tight rock" formations in the foothills of the Rocky Mountains, in giant coal beds throughout Montana, Wyoming, and Alberta, and in very large deposits of methane hydrates in both off-shore and permafrost areas of the world (mostly in Canada and Russia). But this additional gas is very difficult and costly to recover. Some of it, such as deep sea methane hydrates, may not be recoverable economically. While the price of gas is currently high (it tends to follow oil, although not very closely), investors are still unsure whether the price will go high enough and stay there long enough to justify major capital investments in unconventional gas areas.

Undoubtedly the United States will fall back on importing natural gas, as it has oil. Of course, this will reduce U.S. energy independence even further. (A large percentage of U.S. natural gas now is imported from Canada, which is soon likely to protect its own energy security by restricting exports to the United States).

A major alternative source of natural gas is coal. Years ago, it was common to make coal gas (also known as town gas) by destructive distillation of bituminous coal in the absence of air. The coal transformed into coke having numerous industrial and domestic markets. The resulting coal gas was a mixture of about 55 percent hydrogen with a variety of hydrocarbons, some of them quite carcinogenic! Eventually natural gas replaced coal gas, which is now used only in steel making and other processes where the coke is used to reduce metal ores.

During the 1970's, another period of uncertainty over fuel supplies, several technologies were developed to manufacture a small number of fuel gases from coal. These gases included synthetic natural gas (SNG). At least some of the processes, such as the CO_2 Acceptor Process, sequestered the carbon dioxide generated by coal combustion (to produce process heat). These are now called "clean coal" processes. Coal may also be used to produce syngas (hydrogen plus carbon monoxide) and other fuel gases. Since the United States has an estimated 800-year supply of coal at present consumption rates, very likely coal will become a source of synthetic natural gas before 2015 or so as conventional natural gas resources decline.

SNG or syngas can in principle be made from carbonaceous material other than coal. Any carbon-bearing material can be gasified to generate a syngas ($CO + H_2$) mixture. In turn, syngas can be converted into methane, a close approximation to natural gas, or even into liquid fuels. Other than coal, the only carbonaceous feedstock that could make a dent in our huge demand for natural gas is biomass. However, biomass is a widely distributed renewable resource. The logistics (and costs) of collecting and processing biomass raw material on a large scale is a major challenge. Coal was derived from biomass, and fortunately, nature took care of the logistics problem — in only a few million years! The same problem limits the use of biomass to manufacture any fuel (such as synthetic or Fischer-Tropsch diesel) in high volumes.

Coal

As is well documented, the world has enormous reserves of coal. The United States is especially well endowed with it and, unlike oil and natural gas, has used only a fraction of its endowment. Unfortunately also, as is well known and documented, conventional large-scale burning of coal damages the environment. Even with stack gas scrubbing and particulate trapping, the environmental consequences are substantial. Yet, the problem seems likely to become worse before it gets better.

The U.S. Department of Energy forecasts increasing use of coal for power generation through 2025, but has forecast no significant increase in emission controls. There is no likelihood, in DOE's view, of significant carbon sequestration burning coal for power generation before 2025. This is very troubling. Given our economic and technical constraints, and the vast scale on which any energy solution must be implemented, coal may be our best bet. But it will be acceptable only if it is environmentally benign. In other words, we should not burn it as we do today. Instead we should develop to full commercial status several clean coal technologies that have evolved over the three decades since the energy crisis of the 1970s. These technologies offer far more promise than the current dream of converting the whole world to hydrogen.

Fortunately, necessity may drive our choices in the right direction. Hydrogen must be manufactured from another energy source, and producing it on a large scale by known methods defeats the environmental purpose. If it's done by electrolysis of water, the electricity now usually comes from burning fossil fuels. It can be made directly from natural gas, the most popular method today, but natural gas is in short supply.

With primary resources such as oil and natural gas running out (at least in North America), we may be forced to turn to innovative clean coal technologies to meet the large-scale demand forecasted by DoE over the next two decades. Carbon sequestration, regardless of the fuel used, makes more sense than hydrogen. It can be done with lean coal technologies such as fluid bed combustion. CO_2 sequestration is typically in dolomite contained in the bed. Disposal or recycling options for the bed seem relatively straightforward. Another method, partial oxidation with CO_2 capture, is in successful but limited use today. However, it does not make sense to attempt, as some have suggested, sequestration of the carbon before the fuel is burned. Most of the combustion energy in a carbonaceous fuel resides in its carbon content; with that removed (if it could be done), not much that is useful remains!

Nuclear Power

France has demonstrated that nuclear power can provide clean, safe energy to an entire nation of over 60 million people. It could be doing the same in the United States were it not for the fact that decisions about nuclear power and its related waste disposal have become politicized. Unfortunately, because of this, we do not envisage it playing an expanded role in most world economies, including the United States, for at least two decades. Eventually, the waste disposal and proliferation problems will be resolved. Nuclear energy will play an important role in our more distant future — but probably not before 2050 or so.

"Green" Renewable/Sustainable Energy Resources

Notwithstanding all of the enthusiasm for "green, renewable, sustainable," energy sources, near-term implementation of these beyond a local level faces enormous challenges, largely because of the scale on which any meaningful substitution must occur. In addition, some have their own environmental issues. Wind generators are meeting aesthetic resistance in many parts of the country (such as offshore New England). Recently they have been shown to kill considerable numbers of migrating birds, as well as bats and other flying animals.

Wind generators are comparatively capital non-intensive and inexpensive to operate, but staggering numbers of them will be needed to generate the power needed to replace fossil fuels, and the wind does not blow at suitable velocities all of the time. Most wind generation systems to date have averaged only about 11 percent of their design capacity.

Photovoltaic solar generators at present efficiencies require huge land areas and tend to be capital-intensive. Hydroelectric power sites are nearly maxed out. New ones require new dams, submerging additional, perhaps beautiful, countryside — a step that is currently being resisted worldwide (such as China, Belize). Conclusion: renewable energy will make local or even regional contributions to grid power generation, but like biomass, it is unlikely to scale up into a major contributor.

Future Energy Choices, 2005–2100

Conventional energy sources will be in use for many years, albeit at progressively increasing prices. Oil will remain available for many years, even with the increased rates of consumption expected from China, India, and other populous, would-be first-world countries. The stuff is there, but from sources more and more difficult to produce, and therefore more and more costly.

Prices of oil, natural gas, and coal over the next few decades are difficult to predict. They depend on more than geology, ecology, supply and demand, and actual production costs. Global politics have often played a major role in determining oil pricing and actual availability. That is unlikely to change.

Major perturbations in the global supply-demand equation are ever possible, for example, major conflict in the Middle East, or among the states of the former USSR, or for that matter between the United States and Canada. Assuming nothing like that, oil prices will fall back somewhat over the next year or so, perhaps to the U.S. $35 range; then begin a steady increase that will take the price well over U.S. $100 by 2050 or so. (That's in 2005 dollars, no allowances for inevitable changes in exchange rates, general inflation, or the time value of money). However, there will likely be major, unpredictable, short-term "peaks and valleys" in this ramp up as a result of temporary political perturbations.

An increase in crude oil prices is likely to see a parallel increase in gas and coal prices to keep them more or less in line with oil on an equivalent energy content basis. These increases will, of course, drive up the cost of refined end products, like gasoline, which most of us use, either personally or in commercial operations. Factor in the forward margins, and by 2050 the pre-tax prices of gasoline, heating oil, diesel fuel, and jet fuel are likely to reach values that are at least eight times their present levels in 2005 dollars.

This run-up in prices, far more than environmental concerns, will lead to serous consideration of alternate fuels, especially for transportation, and a great focus on fuel conservation. We'll opt for lighter, more fuel-efficient vehicles, just as Europeans do now. Only alternate fuels or alternate vehicle choices that result in tangible fuel and cash savings will be favored. The public on average is happy to talk about a clean environment, but very reluctant to make any personal sacrifice that ensures one. Therefore the drive force for change will be predominantly economic. The initial cost of a vehicle will be much less of a consideration than the cost of fuel on personal cash flow.

If this is to happen in transportation, imagine what it will do for manufacturing. It's time to start attacking the waste in energy usage.

Dr. John R. Wilson is president of The Management Group, TMG/The Management Group in Detroit. He has over 40 years' experience in energy issues, beginning as a professor; with Exxon in fluid coking and flexicoking; then with Shell, where he worked in the Canadian tar sands. The past few years he has advised many companies, including those in the auto industry, on the future of fuels.

Questions

Does it make sense for your company to consider switching to a different fuel source to reduce costs?

Have you calculated what switching would cost?

How do you project the future cost of different types of energy?

7

The Future of Energy in Manufacturing

A rational examination of energy sources for manufacturing in the 1st century: Part 2 of 2 parts.

Dr. John R. Wilson

In Brief

The cost of energy is going to rise. The status of alternative fuel development is very unsettled. Highly touted alternatives, outlined here, are unlikely to see widespread use. The best advice: Avoid wasting energy and develop flexibility to switch fuel sources when necessary.

Future Energy Choices, 2005–2100

As noted in Part 1 of this series, conventional energy sources will be available for many years, but at progressively increasing prices. Besides the increasing difficulty and expense of recovering the stuff, global politics is the wild card — embargos, terrorism, war — who knows what — or where. Expect the rise in prices to also be highly volatile at times. All in all, by 2050 the pretax or wholesale prices of gasoline, heating oil, diesel fuel, and jet fuel are likely to reach values that are at least eight times their present levels in 2005 dollars.

A run-up in prices is much more likely to launch major programs to develop alternative fuels than fickle public concern for environmental sustainability. When our pocketbooks are lightened, we'll get serious about fuel conservation. We'll see alternate fuels, especially for transportation, and opt for lighter, more fuel-efficient vehicles, just as Europeans do now. Expected future fuel costs will influence vehicle selection much more than now. Decisions on manufacturing or business equipment will follow a similar logic.

What are the Options?

One of the characteristics of modern society is that anyone, however well (or poorly) qualified, feels entitled to express an opinion on anything, including topics of intensely technical nature, based on minimal factual knowledge or training. Consequently, a vast amount of misleading nonsense has been written about the benefits of ethanol, hydrogen, or biodiesel as fuels. Some of it is exuberant advocacy; some is wishful thinking; and some of it is based on simple ignorance. The upshot is public confusion when hearing of the latest theory or "breakthrough."

Hydrogen

Hydrogen has recently been the most publicized alternate energy carrier. Is it a realistic option? Hydrogen has been an important industrial gas for many years, but its reported use in the United States has never grown much beyond 10 million metric tons/year (large amounts of non-merchant or captive hydrogen used by the oil industry are not reported). Despite many attempts to use hydrogen as an industrial fuel, it is used only where its unique characteristics are needed — for example, as a reducing agent in metal production; and in the hydrogenation of heavy oils, high-sulfur crude oil products, and certain vegetable oils.

Why is hydrogen not viewed as a good fuel by those who have real-world experience with it?

Hydrogen is not an energy source. It is best viewed as an energy carrier — like electricity, but less convenient. In nature is exists in elemental form only in miniscule amounts, so like electrical power, hydrogen must be manufactured from a true energy source such as natural gas or coal; or generated using another energy carrier such as electricity. Making hydrogen incurs significant added production cost, reducing the efficiency of its overall "energy chain."

Hydrogen can be produced by electrolyzing water (very energy-intensive), by reforming natural gas (that is, by partially oxidizing it and/or by reacting it with steam; much less energy-intensive). Another route is the gasification of coal or other organic material such as wood waste to form syngas ($CO+H_2$), followed by the separation of hydrogen from the co-produced carbon monoxide. According to a recent study by the National Research Council, coal and natural gas offer the most energy-efficient and lowest-cost options, although there are major concerns over the sufficiency of supply of natural gas.[1]

Electrolysis of water is very costly unless exceptionally low-cost power is available "off the grid," perhaps from a captive, dedicated source such as a wind farm (with energy storage to enable continuous production.) Enormous amounts of power are required. Generating by electrolysis enough hydrogen to replace all current U.S. gasoline consumption alone (about one million metric tons/day) would require roughly doubling the existing nationwide generating capacity. But even in modest quantities, producing hydrogen from electricity generated from coal, oil, or natural gas is a very inefficient way to use the energy in these original sources.

Like electricity, hydrogen must be transported from the point of manufacture to the point of use. Many have proposed that hydrogen be made locally, so it need not be transported very far. However, today's technology for small-scale manufacture of hydrogen is locally-owned and operated electrolyzers, or in small-scale methane or methanol reformers, is very inefficient compared with manufacture in large central facilities. Much more development is needed before this route to hydrogen is cost-effective.

Transportation of compressed hydrogen by pipeline, or in liquid form by tube trucks, is also very energy-inefficient because of the very high compression, liquefaction, and pumping costs. At atmospheric pressure, one heavy tube truck would transport a trivial mass of lighter-than-air hydrogen! This lightness is a significant problem. At atmospheric pressure, it has very low heating value per unit volume (320 BTE/ft3 compared to about 1000 from natural gas). Thus, three times the volume of hydrogen must be moved for a given energy requirement, which entails higher pipeline pressures, velocities, or friction losses, therefore taking more energy to convey to the point of use.[2]

For the same reason, conversion of combustion equipment to use hydrogen instead of, say, refinery gas is difficult because much higher gas flows are required in fuel gas handling equipment. Even equipment designed from scratch for hydrogen-rich gas — such as that using coke-oven gas, once common in the steel and iron making industry — presents packaging problems because of the large duct sizes involved.

The very low volumetric energy density of hydrogen (such as kWh/m3) makes it troublesome for vehicle design, especially in small, light-duty vehicles that already have a fuel system "packaging" problem. Storing enough hydrogen to provide a reasonable driving range is problematic. For example, GM's current best solution for storing 8Kg of compressed hydrogen (10,000 psi) is three cylindrical 11-in. diameter tanks that run the length of its Sequel concept vehicle beneath the floor. This system is heavy, resulting in a considerable fuel economy penalty. Located under the floor, a small leak and fire would do maximum damage to the vehicle's occupants. An alternative, storing hydrogen in metallic hydrides is also limited by the basic physics of the materials.

Larger vehicles, buses, long-haul trucks, or railroad locomotives can accommodate larger fuel tanks with less sacrifice of space or fuel economy. However, hydrogen, like helium, has a remarkable ability to leak from pressurized equipment as anyone who has used it in an industrial context knows only too well. Road vehicles, regardless of size, will not be immune to this problem!

In general, except for industrial applications such as hydrogenation for which there is no alternative, hydrogen is a less than optimal fuel. The advantage of having no final combustion emissions (other than a relatively low level of nitrogen oxides) is offset by the processes used to manufacture it. Reforming, generating power for electrolysis of water, and coal gasification are energy-intensive and do generate plenty of emissions. Unless equipped with carbon sequestration or other emissions control technology, they can easily result in higher CO_2 or other emissions than direct-burning an alternative fuel. It can easily take far more energy to make and transport hydrogen than is obtainable from it at the point of use.

As a chemical feedstock, hydrogen is great because it is unique. As a fuel, it is a loser.

Non-Hydrogen Fuel Gases

Natural gas, the "golden fuel," is much more convenient to use and less environmentally damaging than conventional coal, but the United States and Canada are running short of it. That's bad news for compressed natural gas (CNG), liquefied natural gas (LNG), or other more specialized hydrocarbon gases, such as propane or butane. They are often derived from natural gas. Imports of LNG in tankers are increasing. It is converted to gaseous form at the receiving marine terminal, and used to augment normal natural gas supplies. Given the projection of tight supplies, any plans to increase demand for natural gas seem inappropriate, at least until new exploration and recovery efforts in North America have begun to show progress.

Efforts are growing in both the United States and Canada to find and produce more gas both from deep offshore gas fields, and from coal beds. Production of coal bed methane uses huge volumes of ground water, often turning it high in sulfur, a major environmental concern. In several locations in the United States and Canada, notably the western foothills of the Rockies, natural gas exists in tight rock formations. These are costly to work. They must be fractured hydraulically to release the gas, which requires expensive equipment and considerable energy.

Methane hydrates are a big potential source of methane, but recovery from them is tough. Vast amounts are believed to lie beneath the oceans off the United States and Japan and below the permafrost in the Arctic, in Canada, and in Russia. Under the ocean they're in layers covered by a layer of silt at depths of 500–2000 meters. In permafrost, they typically lie at the interface between the permanently frozen zone and the normally unfrozen material below it. Here they may be easier to recover, but most deposits are a thin layer of solid material extending over a very large area, and very temperature and pressure sensitive. A test well, Malik, in the Canadian Northwest Territories, funded by several nations, has generated interesting results, but no proven, accepted, cost-effective technology to recover methane from hydrates yet exists.

Note on global warming: Warming the ocean and melting the permafrost may release methane from thawing hydrates. Since methane is a much more effective global warming agent than carbon dioxide, this positive feedback loop could be accelerating it.

Synthetic Natural Gas (SNG)

SNG and natural gas, functionally identical, burn the same. Technology to manufacture SNG from coal is in an advanced stage of development. Technology to extract SNG from other organic material, including dry municipal waste isn't as far developed.

Coal

Coal is abundant in the United States and elsewhere in the world. DOE forecasts a major increase in coal-fired power stations through 2025. But it burns dirty. To protect the environment it should be burnt cleanly. When coal is burned directly, treating stack gas only partially controls emissions. "Clean Coal" methods such as fluid bed combustion, with carbon dioxide capture, not only improve emissions control, they maximize the heat released from the fuel. Money now spent on hydrogen would be far better spent to improve this technology either to generate heat or to manufacture synthetic natural gas.

Synthetic fuels have been made from coal since the 1940s. Germany produced fuel this way during World War II. South Africa and New Zealand have successfully produced fuels this way, if very expensively. Having coal but little oil quickly fires the imagination. Distilling coal can produce liquids directly. Gasifying coal can produce syngas (or even synthetic natural gas). Fischer-Tropsch catalytic conversion of the gas can result in, for example, synthetic diesel, synthetic avgas and gasoline, and even synthetic oxyfuels such as methanol.

"Clean Coal" technology confers more benefits than sequestering CO_2. Coal has a deserved reputation for environmental damage when mined, between mine site and point of use, when used, and afterward. All of these issues have to be addressed, and they are being addressed. We're close to a truly "clean" suite of coal technologies, providing "clean" liquid and gaseous fuels. At current consumption rates, U.S. coal reserves are somewhere between 400 and 800 years, a longevity likely to become much shorter with clean coal.

Biofuels and Synthetic Fuels

Interest is keen in alternate liquid fuels, mostly from non-petroleum sources. Ethanol, the best known alternate, is derived primarily from corn starch by fermentation and distillation. Another alternative is biodiesel, normally a blend of vegetable oil methyl esters and conventional diesel. "Sunfuels" are mostly biomass-derived synthetic diesel, but can also be made from natural gas. Both biodiesel and ethanol are commercially available now.

Synthetic diesel is being produced in developmental quantities by several major producers selling it "invisibly" as diesel blending stock. Qatar has funded several large commercial synthetic diesel projects using its vast reserves of natural gas as the feedstock. "Sunfuels" are in a much earlier stage of development, but probably will be a force in the market by 2015–2020, more exciting to Europeans than North Americans.

Ethanol

Ethanol and methanol are chemical feedstocks that have found uses as motor fuels. Pure methanol is a racing fuel. Ethanol is typically blended with gasoline (10–15 percent ethanol). As motor fuels, both are limited by relatively low energy density compared with gasoline and diesel. Its primary fuel value is an emission control additive for gasoline, replacing MTBE (which contaminates groundwater when gasoline tanks leak). Ethanol is normally used as an industrial fuel only if there is no alternative.

Unfortunately ethanol is one of the least energy-efficient fuels available if all of the energy involved in its manufacture is accounted for. It looks much better than it is by treating the solar energy accumulated in the feedstock as a "freebie," ignoring the large land area required to collect it. That sets up an unfair comparison with fossil fuels (whose energy also comes from solar energy absorbed by the original organic material). Ethanol needs federal or state subsidies to make it economically viable as either fuel or gasoline additive. Technology is under development to produce ethanol from cellulosic biomass (such as wood waste, farm residues, and even purpose-grown crops) by acid hydrolysis and then fermentation. The first small-scale commercial operation was only recently commissioned (by Logen Corporation in Ottawa). Proof whether this will lower cost must await large-scale production.

Methanol

Methanol is a widely used chemical feedstock. It can be made from a variety of sources, including biomass, but usually from natural gas — the much lower cost natural gas from overseas. As a fuel, methanol shows promise in direct methanol fuel cells (not hydrogen). These are refuelable, and are currently available to power cell phones or laptop computers. As a motor fuel, methane's low energy content makes it a poor choice except in exceptionally high octane, high compression competition engines.

Methanol can readily be reformed into hydrogen. Methanol reformers for possible hydrogen manufacture require a methanol-water mixture, a good hydrogen carrier because both methanol and water contain high levels of hydrogen (12.5 wt% and 11 wt%, respectively). However, at 25 percent, methane or natural gas is a better hydrogen carrier.

Biodiesel

Directly burning vegetable oils, like soybean oil or canola (rapeseed oil), in diesel engines is not recommended. Fatty acid triglycerides in them can corrode engines and fuel systems. To remove all the triglycerides, almost all commercial biodiesel reacts vegetable oils with 10–15 percent methyl alcohol to produce fatty acid methyl esters (ethyl and other alcohols can also be used). The triglycerides come out as glycerol.

The actual fuel burnt blends 2–20 percent of this "straight" biodiesel with conventional diesel fuel. These blends reduce particulate, CO, and HC emissions. The jury is still out on NOx. Biodiesel blends are widely available in the central and southern Midwestern United States, but not in northern tier states because of inferior cold weather properties. However, canola-based biodiesel blended with lower-viscosity D-1 petroleum diesel is widely used in Canada as a winter fuel. Biodiesel blends evaluated for gas turbine use are generally more costly than jet-type fuels. They also exhibit a few technical problems, notably lack of oxidative stability, which is also the reason they have limited appeal as an industrial fuel.

Like ethanol, biodiesel is not an energy-efficient fuel if the energy in the ingoing raw material (soybeans or soybean oil) is accounted for — as it should be. In some situations, simply burning the beans or the extracted oil for heat would make more sense. However, most biodiesel in the United States is a byproduct of making soybean animal feed (to extract the protein in the soybean), so it's not subject to the same stringent thermal analysis as a fossil fuel.

Expansive use of biodiesel would require major restructuring of the agriculture industry. Soybean oil, the major raw material in the United States, is already in strong demand for non-fuel uses. Adding fuel demand to it would require a large increase in acreage dedicated to soybeans, possibly displacing other key crops. Shifting all current distillate production toward biodiesel isn't desirable technically either. Biodiesel is a low-BTU fuel best used as an additive.

Synthetic Diesel Fuel

Distilled from crude oil, like gasoline, conventional diesel fuel is one of the liquids generally referred to as distillate fuels or "middle distillates." Road diesel fuels have historically contained high levels of sulfur (currently regulated to 300 ppm or less). Marine, locomotive, and industrial diesel fuels often contain far more sulfur, but are increasingly coming under regulation. Sulfur is responsible for much of diesel's particulate and SOx emissions, as well as the lovely smell of diesel exhaust. Actual sulfur levels in road diesel have fallen in anticipation of tougher regulations, now averaging less than 100 ppm in the United States and Canada. By 2006, EPA-regulated levels will drop to 15 ppm in the United States, with similar levels in Canada. European levels will become even lower at 10 ppm. Many European countries already sell fuel below this level.

Ultra-low sulfur levels trim exhaust emission. The new Euro IV diesel emission regulations and those in force in the United States and Canada by 2007–2008 will require "clean diesel" engines using high pressure injection (common rail or unit injector), low-sulfur fuel, and , probably, exhaust after-treatment such as NOx and/or particulate trapping. (California, as usual, led the way on these regulations). Concern is serious that these regulations will drive diesel engines from at least the automotive market, which would be counterproductive. Diesels, especially if using biomass-based fuels, are one of the best bets to improve overall U.S. fuel economy. What fuels can achieve these 2008 standards? Very low sulfur fuels, also low in aromatics content.

The level of aromatic compounds in standard distillate fuels depends on the refinery and crude oil used to make them. Aromatics contribute to particulate emissions. They may cause potentially carcinogenic and currently non-regulated emissions, like formaldehyde and naphthalene. Refiners, feeling considerable pressure to reduce aromatics levels, are turning to synthetic diesel fuels.

Synthetic diesel fuels are made from supplies of natural gas or refinery gas (for example) that now have no market, perhaps because volumes are too small to justify refining into pipeline gas, or no collection system is nearby. To make synthetic diesel fuel, natural gas is reformed or partially oxidized into a mixture of hydrogen and oxygen and then passed over a Fischer-Tropsch catalyst at elevated temperature. A mix of diesel-range hydrocarbons come out. These must usually be refined by distillation, but they are very low in sulfur and aromatics, the ideal diesel fuel for the coming tight emissions regime. Currently produced in small volumes, most synthetic diesel sold is blended into conventional petroleum diesel.

Soon very large amounts of synthetic diesel will be available from Qatar, Nigeria, and similar locations, from natural gas not easy to economically transport. Commercialization of this technology is being led there and elsewhere by "Big Oil" (like BP, Conoco-Phillips, and Shell).

Expect synthetic diesel to be a major player in the post-2007 clean diesel markets around the world.

Sunfuels: Biomass-Based Diesel

Sunfuels are made by gasifying biomass to form a syngas, which is converted to a diesel-like fuel by Fischer-Tropsch processing. If biomass provides much of the energy to process a biomass feedstock, synthetic diesel made this way can legitimately be labeled a biofuel. Biodiesel, obviously a biofuel, is popular with Europeans, and they are becoming more interested in synthetic diesel fuels made from biomass of various kinds. Numerous possible raw materials are being assessed.

"Sunfuels," properly used, refers to synthetic diesel manufacture from biomass, but equivalent to that obtained from natural gas. With any biomass, the logistics of collecting voluminous crops to a central location for processing are formidable. However, the big perceived advantage of biomass — that it effectively re-uses the CO_2 that is produced in combustion of the fuel — will drive its adoption in countries that believe elimination of CO_2 emissions to be the key to controlling global warming. Sunfuel synthetic diesel is greener than biodiesel because it is all biomass-based, while biodiesel is blended with petroleum-based diesel.

Sunfuel synthetic diesel, sulfur-free and very low in aromatics, has great promise as a future road fuel. In addition, minor variations in the Fischer-Tropsch process can control oxygen content in the product fuel. That could also help control emissions.

Last, but Certainly not Least — Electricity

Electricity, like hydrogen, is not an energy source but an energy carrier — generated traditionally from energy sources like natural gas, coal and oil, or from hydro and nuke. Converting fossil fuels to electricity typically captures 35–40 percent of the energy in them, depending on fuel selection, plant design, and age. Increasing this energy yield would have a huge impact.

Electricity is a far more convenient and efficient carrier of energy than hydrogen, so it makes little sense to convert it to hydrogen. When made by burning fossil fuels spewing emissions, neither is environmentally benign. The only difference between creating environmental damage at a carrier's point of generation or its point of use is which area suffers the most locally.

"Green" power generation methods include fuel cells, solar photovoltaic generators, wind generators, and hydroelectric generators capturing energy from ocean tidal currents and flowing rivers. These are non-polluting at the point of power generation. However, everything impacts the environment. The things have to be built, installed, and power transmitted from them. Windmills kill birds and bats. Aesthetically, some like their looks; some think they're ugly. Solar collectors covering huge tracts of land are no prettier than most conventional power plants. Anything that generates electricity generally has a downside somewhere, so choices must be carefully considered.

Most alternative sources of electrical power are now small and local, kilowatt- or megawatt-sized, rather than gigawatt-sized, like conventional power plants. They may keep running when the grid goes down, like auxiliary power now, but ties to the grid go both ways. If fueled, they usually produce power intermittently, when the sun shines or the wind blows. And it takes a lot of them to add up to a gigawatt.

Large fuel cells have been built and operated for years as auxiliary power generators, although seldom powered by hydrogen. Industry is planning several hydrogen fuel cells, up to 200 MW, burning by-product hydrogen from large electrolytic chlorine-producing facilities. Transport energy of the hydrogen is negligible, so it is often thought of (wrongly) as "free," but they will be a blip in total power generation.

Probably the best hope for the future large-scale electricity generation in reincarnation of nuclear power. Its problems associated with waste handling and proliferation have to be solved first, but at present, we're not practically focused on them. Neither DOE nor the nuclear industry appears to be prepared to deal with the problem right now.

Costs

The costs of most new substitute fuels are not yet well documented. Only the cost of biodiesel is well established (as are its federal and state subsidies). The costs of synthetic diesel and biomass-based sunfuels are not yet well established, but are somewhat higher than conventional diesel. However the cost of conventional diesel is forecast to increase — slowly — so this disadvantage may not last long, and won't be significant if the somewhat lower lubricity of very low sulfur fuels can be offset by suitable additives (one of which is biodiesel!).

What Does All of This Mean for Manufacturers?

Sharp energy prices of the past two years may have some downward adjustment in the next one to two years, but long-term, the trend is upward. Within five or more years, expect conventional energy supplies to become much more costly. In addition, within a decade or so, regional and national supply shortages of natural gas and refined oil products are likely to trigger force majeure clauses in long-term supply contracts.

While there is no immediate need to switch to alternate fuels, significant energy users should develop strategic energy plans that include alternatives. The selection made will depend on a number of factors such as:

- The amount and nature of fuel or energy now used and projected to be used
- The type, projected availability, and projected cost of conventional fuels currently in use
- The type, projected availability, and projected cost of any alternative fuel to be considered
- The age and efficiency of energy-using equipment currently in place
- The capital cost of upgrading or replacing equipment for alternative fuel use
- Any overriding litigation-driven or emotion-driven preferences, that is for the use of carbon-neutral fuels (biomass-based) or for those that contribute to a reduction in U.S. energy imports (biomass-based, domestic coal-based, methane hydrate-based).

The issue to watch planning future energy strategy is the projected, future availability of the various energy alternatives. Biofuels and hydrogen are unlikely to prevail as more than special-case or local supplies. They are either too inefficient or not reliable enough for widespread use. Hydrogen is energy inefficient to produce and now must be made from resources that we fear will run out! Biofuels of any kind made from biomass, were demand to approach the level of conventional energy today, would require quantities of organic materials that cannot be grown in sufficient quantity by our present agricultural systems and technology.

That leaves a continuation of using oil and gas as we know it today, synthetic fuels made from natural gas and coal (with, perhaps, a small contribution from biomass) and electricity, powered increasingly by nuclear power and by "clean coal."

Fortunately, the world is not yet out of energy. For the next several decades, the energy future looks like a much more expensive version of the energy present, at least until a breakthrough comes along. So far, despite claims by everyone from Jeremy Rifkin to General Motors, we do not have it.

Dr. John R. Wilson is president of The Management Group, and TMG/Energy in Detroit and is closely associated with NextEnergy Center, a Detroit areas not-for-profit organization that is focused on encouraging and enabling the development, commercialization and use of alternate energy technologies. He has over 40 years' experience in energy issues, beginning as a professor; with Exxon in fluid coking and Flexicoking; then on to Shell, where he worked in the Canadian Oil Sands. The past few years he has advised many companies including those in the auto industry, on the future of fuels. Dr. Wilson is busy completing a book on "Energizing our Future" with co-author Griffin Burgh.

Notes

1. National Research Council, National Academy of Engineering, "The Hydrogen Economy: Opportunities, Costs, Barriers and R&D Needs," Michael Ramage, Chairman, available from the National Academy at: www.nap.edu/books/0309091632/html/.
2. See Ulf Bossel, Baldur Eliasson, and Gordon Taylor, www.efcf.com/reports/E08.pdf.

Questions

Do any of the alternative fuels gaining in popularity make sense for your operations?

Are you looking at projected future availability of these fuels?

Do you have a strategic energy plan?

Section III

EPA Case Studies

8

3M Lean Six Sigma and Sustainability

From "Pollution Prevention Pays" to Sustainability at 3M

In Brief

For three decades, 3M has been focusing on preventing pollution in the first place rather than removing or treating it later. A Lean Six Sigma approach is now an integral part of achieving goals of sustainability.

3M is widely recognized as a pioneer in corporate pollution prevention. In 2005, 3M's Pollution Prevention Pays (3P) program celebrated its 30th anniversary. Over the last 31 years, the program has prevented more than 2.6 billion pounds of pollutants and saved more than $1 billion based on aggregated data from the first year of each 3P project. The 3P program helps prevent pollution at the source — in products and manufacturing processes — rather than removing it after it has been created. 3P projects typically focus on product reformulation, process modification, equipment redesign, or recycling and reuse of waste materials. As of 2006, 3M employees worldwide have completed more than 6,300 3P projects.

3P is a key element of 3M's environmental strategy and in moving toward sustainability. 3P has achieved that status based on the belief that a prevention approach is more environmentally effective, technically sound, and economical than conventional pollution controls. The 3P program targets key environmental metrics: VOC emissions, TRI releases, water releases, waste generation, energy consumption and greenhouse gas emissions. With 3P and other environmental management systems in place, 3M continues to commit to environmental reductions and become a sustainable growth corporation-one whose products and processes have a minimal impact on the environment.

3M's focus on sustainability and sustainable development has increased in recent years (www.3m.com/sustainability). 3M produces a corporate sustainability report using the Global Reporting Initiative guidelines. In 2007, 3M was once again selected for inclusion into the Dow Jones Sustainability Index and named as the Industrial Goods and Services Sector Leader. 3M has been included in the index and named leader of its sector since its inception.

Lean Six Sigma at 3M

3M has also been a pioneer in the use of Lean Six Sigma methods and tools to improve operations and quality. (Lean Six Sigma is a process-improvement methodology and a collection of statistical tools designed to reduce process variation and improve product quality.) While Lean Six Sigma activity had been underway throughout 3M for several years, 3M launched a corporate-wide Lean Six Sigma initiative in February 2001, with senior leadership support. As of 2006, more than 55,000 salaried employees at 3M have been trained in Lean Six Sigma processes and methodologies, and more than 45,000 Lean Six Sigma projects have been initiated or closed. Lean and Six Sigma methodologies provide a strong focus for enterprise wide implementation and are now viewed as basic components of 3M's corporate culture. 3M's Lean Six Sigma vision, "Achieving Breakthrough Performance for our Customers, Employees and Shareholders," is firmly rooted in the company's long history and culture of innovation.

Lean Six Sigma and Environmental Goals

3M Environmental, Health, and Safety managers view Lean Six Sigma as a powerful tool for achieving current and future corporate EHS and sustainability goals. The company noted that while Lean Six Sigma projects focused on improving operational efficiency and product yield, direct reductions in energy use, air emissions, waste reduction, greenhouse gas emissions, and other environmental impacts also coincided. With its 2000–2005 Environmental *Targets* (ET'05), 3M began tracking whether 3P projects have a Lean Six Sigma component by including a check box on the 3P project form. In 2006, more than 70 percent of all 3P projects relied upon Lean Six Sigma methods, at least in part.

Lean Six Sigma has helped to reinvigorate the 3P program at 3M, yielding impressive results. In 2000, 3M set ET'05 goals to address environmental issues through eco-efficiency and pollution prevention metrics. They were complemented by individual business unit goals that incorporated product life cycle management within the unit's strategic plan. The ET'05 goals and results are summarized below.

Environmental Goals (2000–2005)

	Goal	Results
Reduce volatile air emissions indexed to net sales	25%	61%
Reduce U.S. Environmental Protection Agency Toxic Release Inventory (TRI) Releases indexed to net sales	50%	64%
Improve energy efficiency (energy use indexed to net sales)	20%	27%
Reduce waste indexed to net sales	25%	30%
Double the number of Pollution Prevention Pays (3P) projects from the previous five-year period from 194 to 400 projects	400	1262

In 2005, 3M established a new set of corporate environmental goals from 2005 through 2010 (ET'10), as follows.[1]
- Reduce volatile air emissions by 25 percent.
- Improve energy efficiency by 20 percent.
- Reduce waste by 20 percent.
- Implement 800 3P projects.

Lean Six Sigma is anticipated to play a major role in 3M's efforts to achieve the ET'10 goals. Lean Six Sigma has become a powerful engine supporting expanded pollution prevention activity and effectiveness at 3M. Given Lean Six Sigma's focus on involving different voices through the use of cross-functional teams, personnel with environmental expertise are often involved in Lean Six Sigma project teams. "Voice of Customer" interviews and survey results also reflect increasing interest in environmental performance results. As the pace of Lean Six Sigma activities increase at 3M, much of the waste and variation targeted for elimination in Lean Six Sigma projects will bring environmental improvements on their coattails. Lean Six Sigma control plans and post-project audits will help to ensure that these achievements endure.

Lean Six Sigma and Environment, Health, and Safety Operations at 3M

Since 2001, 3M's Environmental, Health, and Safety Operations (EH&SO) organization has deployed Lean Six Sigma to improve corporate EHS services and activities. As of February 2007, the EH&SO organization had two Lean Six Sigma black belts and a master black belt focused on corporate EHS projects and coaching (for approximately 100 team members). All EHS team members are required to become Lean Six Sigma green belts and to lead at least one Six Sigma project. EHS team members receive two weeks of Lean Six Sigma green belt training, and coaching is provided by black belts. EHS Lean Six Sigma projects have focused on topics ranging from compliance or due diligence activities to data collection and management to communications.

While some of the Lean Six Sigma projects launched by 3M's EH&SO organization have a positive return on investment using conventional cost reduction-value creation measures, many projects are justified by driving 3M toward sustainable practices and enhancing 3M's reputation.

In addition to the Lean Six Sigma projects launched by the EH&SO organization, multiple Lean Six Sigma projects are undertaken by EHS personnel at 3M's numerous manufacturing and research and development (R&D) facilities worldwide.

3M Innovation and Sustainability

In 3M's sustainability journey Lean Six Sigma has driven projects in a number of business processes, including R&D and manufacturing, and with customers. 3M's large R&D operations offer both fertile ground for 3P pollution prevention projects and a talented laboratory for developing products and processes aligned with the company's commitment to sustainable development. Going forward, 3M expects to continue capitalizing on these R&D resources, in addition to continuing a strong focus on manufacturing excellence, reduced variability and increasing speed for customers. Lean Six Sigma is anticipated to play a continued central role in driving breakthrough improvements and products that sustain 3M's leadership in innovation and sustainability.

Note

1. All goals are indexed to net sales, except for the goal about the number of 3P projects. 3M had a TRI release reduction goal under ET'05 program. Since most of 3M's TRI releases are volatile air emissions, these releases are addressed by 3M's volatile air emissions reduction goal under the ET'10 program.

Questions

Does your company attempt to reduce pollution at the source?

Is a continuous improvement strategy part of your sustainability efforts?

Are sustainability goals part of R&D as well as manufacturing?

Baxter Healthcare Corporation

9

In Brief

Through the use of value stream mapping, Baxter Healthcare is identifying the destination, use, value, and waste of water used in its production processes. These efforts are identifying opportunities for saving thousands of gallons of water as well as thousands of dollars.

General Introduction

In 2001, Baxter Healthcare Corporation, a worldwide leader in the manufacture of global medical products, was concerned that its environmental footprint per unit output, a key benchmark of efficiency, was growing. To combat this, the company adopted a host of business and manufacturing methods. One worked: Lean Manufacturing. As Baxter began to see waste generation drop with the deployment of Lean, the environmental engineering group realized that environmental improvement was often an unintended benefit of Lean Manufacturing. In order to maximize this benefit, this group began to seek ways to further integrate environmental metrics and performance into traditional Lean Manufacturing tools.

Using Lean practices, sometimes integrated with an environmental focus, the company was able to double in size and revenue while keeping its total waste generation close to 1996 levels. Baxter has been so successful at reducing waste that many of its largest facilities are now classified as small quantity or conditionally exempt small quantity generators under EPA's hazardous waste regulations.

This case study highlights a water value stream mapping (VSM) exercise held at a Southeastern United States facility.

Baxter's Key Lesson Learned

Based on a value stream mapping (VSM) event held at this facility, as well as other similar events, Baxter has developed a number of key lessons for making value stream mapping work:

- The targeted aspect (energy, water, materials, etc.) should be linked to facility challenges and the company strategic plan. For example, if the facility has boilers or uses steam or distilled water, it should find opportunities in water and its associated energy. In ISO 14001 terms, the facility should be targeting one of its environmentally significant aspects.
- A cross-functional team is essential to successfully identifying and understanding the challenge. Upper management support is critical for the follow-up on implementation.
- Good, accurate data is also essential. Data can be gathered in a number of creative ways, as simple as a bucket and stopwatch (water), a clip-on current reader (energy), or a portable flow meter for water discharge. Many utilities provide these services for low or no cost.
- If necessary, bring in expertise. If expertise is not available in-house, then use the many free resources that states provide, such as energy experts, water engineers, etc.
- Do not rely on lean consultants alone. Lean is a way of seeing and thinking, not merely a set of tools. Lean consultants can be a great source of tools and training, but a facility cannot truly learn lean without living lean.
- The metrics chosen should be appropriate to measure progress in the targeted processes. The team must be ready to revise or scrap an ineffective metric.
- Environmental personnel should be given the same representation and responsibilities as other staff. For example, if an operations manager has to provide a monthly report, so should the EHS officer. The environmental staff is an integral part of the team.

Baxter Manufacturing Plant, Southeastern United States

Baxter's solution plants, which manufacture flexible-container IV and peritoneal dialysis products, often use large quantities of water and energy. With steadily increasing energy costs and increasing pressure on clean water supplies, these facilities are encouraged by Baxter's corporate vice president of manufacturing to reduce water and energy consumption. Plants were specifically encouraged to perform a "utilities value stream map."

The plant selected for this study is one of Baxter's largest facilities. The facility has received numerous honors, including the Shingo Award for Manufacturing Excellence. In its quest for "Perfect Processes," the plant actively uses lean practices.

Because the plant gets its water from its own wells, employees incorrectly assumed that water had little cost associated with it, thus ignoring the energy use and costs of pumping, storing, heating, filtering, and disposing of water. Baxter views water waste as an indicator of other costly inefficiencies. For example, water waste is often directly tied to excessive energy consumption.

Creating the Current State Value Stream Map for Water

To attack the water waste challenge, managers chose to use value stream mapping (VSM), one of four key approaches Baxter uses to incorporate environmental metrics into lean practices (see appendix). This marked the first time that VSM was used at this facility to track a material resource—in this case, water—through the entire production process. To create the VSM, a diverse team was chosen that included utility and water experts as well as maintenance, production and EHS personnel. The value stream maps and associated implementation plans were developed over a three-day event.

The first day began with introductions, followed by an explanation of the format and process of the VSM event. Then, the mapping began. Using sticky notes, the team graphically walked through the entire production process, highlighting water usage and major processing steps. The first pass of mapping was high-level and general; each subsequent pass would add more detail and refinement. During the second round of mapping, the major processes were broken down into subprocesses. Then, using the expertise of the participants, the water volumes, cycle-times, value-added calculations (e.g., cost of pumping the water to the next step) and other relevant information were added to the map, with costs normalized per 1,000 gallons. The team also listed the "triggers" that caused each process step to initiate (e.g., an empty tank might trigger a rinsing/flushing process step).

In addition, the team emphasized differences between what should happen in theory versus the actual practices on the floor. For example, although standard operating procedure (SOP) was to rinse the floors and surface areas of certain rooms following a shift, often the entire room, including the walls, was rinsed, thus wasting water. Emphasizing the difference between procedure and practice allowed waste to be better identified, with some SOPs tagged for further evaluation at a later date. The result of the mapping was the current state value stream map, a credible outline of the destination, use, value, and waste of the water throughout the production process.

Metrics

The team then deliberated on which indicators and metrics to use to evaluate the water usage. They understood that the correct choice of metrics was critical to the VSM's success. The choice of indicators and metrics had to be consistent with Baxter's strategic objectives as well as capable of measuring progress relative to the opportunities developed through the VSM. For this VSM, the key metrics included costs (e.g., the dollar value of energy used to process the water) and water volumes. The amount of water withdrawn from the on-site well versus the amount of product produced was an additional efficiency metric. In addition, the team had to be prepared to adjust or replace these indicators and metrics if they proved ineffective in practice.

Ranking Opportunities

Through the VSM, the team identified and prioritized 96 opportunities, with many graphically represented by starbursts. These opportunities were categorized by the estimated length of time for implementation (e.g., 6 months, 12 months, 24 months) and potential for improvement. Then, they were visually plotted on a grid with the magnitude of the potential benefit on the Y-axis and ease of implementation on the X-axis. After all the starbursts had been evaluated on this grid, the results were transferred onto various "future state" timetables, to prioritize the opportunities and plan for their implementation. Generally, starbursts that can be implemented within six months require little or no capital investment (although some may require further analysis to accurately gauge potential benefits). These starbursts are often the first priority for implementation, because of their high return on investment (ROI).

Then, the team created three future state VSMs (6 months, 12 months, and 24 months) that incorporated the prioritized opportunities. New teams were formed to coordinate the changes. These teams were composed of a mix of personnel that had appropriate knowledge of the processes involved as well as a solid awareness of how each chosen process fit within Baxter's strategic objectives. As some members of these new teams did not participate in creating the VSMs, (for example, quality personnel) it was important to ensure that they all understood the strategy and methods behind the VSM effort. The teams developed specific timelines for implementing the changes using traditional lean techniques, like kaizen.

Projected Savings

At the end of the event, Baxter had an action plan that should save 170,000 gallons of water per day and $17,000 within three months, with little or no capital investment. The plan also eliminated the need to expand the plant's wastewater treatment plant. Also, since the event, both the head utilities manager and plant manager have been promoted to positions in the corporate office.

Because Baxter makes medical products, changes in a production process might conflict with FDA requirements. Any costs associated with pursuing an adjustment in those requirements would affect the production change's ROI, and thus, its implementation priority.

Questions

Are you looking at efficient use of water as well as efficient use of energy?

Have you applied value stream mapping to tracking water use?

Do you know how to gather data for tracking water use? Do you know which metrics to use?

10

General Motors Corporation

In Brief

Lean initiatives have long been a part of strategy at General Motors. Through a wide range of efforts, GM is using these initiatives to achieve sustainability goals, ranging from less use of packaging, less use of harmful solvents, reduced need for painting and reduced production of waste.

Background

General Motors Corporation (GM) has one of the most wide-spread lean manufacturing initiatives in place in the United States GM grew interested in lean manufacturing in the early 1980s, as it examined elements of the Toyota Production System that had been adopted by several Japanese auto manufacturers.

In 1994, GM and Toyota formed a joint venture called the New United Motor Manufacturing, Inc. (NUMMI) to pioneer implementation of lean methods at an automotive manufacturing plant in the United States. Compared to a conventional GM plant, NUMMI was able to cut assembly hours per car from 31 to 19 and assembly defects per 100 cars from 135 to 45. By the early 1990s, the success of NUMMI, among other factors, made it increasingly clear that lean manufacturing offers potent productivity, product quality, and profitability advantages over traditional mass production, batch-and-queue systems. By 1997, the "big three" U.S. auto manufacturers indicated that they intend to implement their own lean systems across all of their manufacturing operations.

Since the early 1990's, GM has worked actively to integrate lean manufacturing and environmental initiatives through its PICOS Program (described below). In addition, GM's WE CARE (Waste Elimination and

Cost Awareness Reward Everyone) Program complements lean implementation efforts at GM facilities, as many projects result in both operational and environment improvements. The WE CARE Program is a corporate initiative that formalizes design for the environment and pollution prevention efforts into a team-oriented approach.

Example: Lean Projects and Results

Saturn Kanban Implementation

Saturn's Spring Hill, Tennessee automotive manufacturing plant receives more than 95 percent of its parts in reusable containers. Many of these reusable containers also serve as kanban, or signals for when more parts are needed in a particular process area. This "kanban"-type system eliminates tons of packaging wastes each year and reduces the space, cost, and energy needs of managing such wastes.

Saturn has also implemented electronic kanban with some suppliers, enabling the suppliers to deliver components "just-in-time" for assembly. For example, seating systems are delivered to the shop floor in the order in which they will be installed. Saturn also found that improved "first-time" quality and operational improvements linked to lean production systems reduced paint solvent usage by 270 tons between 1995 and 1996.

Fairfax Assembly Paint Booth Cleaning

At GM's Fairfax Assembly Plant, paint booths were originally cleaned every other day (after production) to prevent stray drops or chips of old paint from attaching onto subsequent paint jobs. It was discovered, however, that the automated section of the painting operations really only needed to be cleaned once a week, as long as the cleaning was thorough, and larger holes were cut in the floor grating to allow for thicker paint accumulations. The reduction in cleaning frequency facilitates improvements in the process "up-time" and flow. As an additional benefit, through this and other more efficient cleaning techniques, use of purge solvent decreased by 3/8 of a gallon per vehicle. When combined with reductions achieved by solvent recycling, VOC emissions from purge solvent reduced by 369 tons in the first year following these adjustments.

Application of Lean Methods to Administrative Processing in the Purchasing Group

In addition to applying lean thinking to manufacturing processes, GM has looked at ways to lean its internal administrative processes. For example, GM's purchasing group investigated the company's Request for Quote (RFQ) processes by which supplier products are sought. Because each RFQ has to include a detailed listing of system requirements, RFQ's under the prior paper-based system could be quite large, ranging in size (in total paper "thickness") from 3/4 of an inch to 6 inches thick.

Upon applying a value stream mapping and analysis, GM identified a number of ways in which this process produced an excessive amount of waste. Not only did it require GM to purchase and use a great deal of paper, but also incurred costs and used raw materials associated with printing and packaging, in addition to cost and energy required to deliver each package to each potential supplier.

GM's solution was to transform the RFQ process into an electronic-based system that is not only paperless, but that avoids the additional costs and waste associated with printing, packaging, and shipping each RFQ. Using an internet-based system called Covisint, GM is able to improve procurement efficiency while lowering costs by saving time and eliminating waste. By distributing RFQ's electronically, GM estimates that the company will save at least two tons of paper each year.

Lean Enterprise Supply Chain Development

In the early 1990s, GM realized that it was not sufficient to just lean GM's operations, as GM (and the customer) directly bears the costs of supplier waste, inefficiency, delays, and defects. GM assigned a group of engineers to work more closely with its suppliers to reduce costs and to improve product quality and on-time delivery.

This effort has involved over 150 supplier development engineers conducting lean implementation workshops called Purchased Input Concept Optimization with Suppliers (PICOS). As part of PICOS, small teams of GM engineers visit GM suppliers for several days to conduct training on lean methods and to lead a focused kaizen-type rapid improvement event. Follow-up was conducted with the suppliers at three and six months to determine if productivity improvements had been maintained, and to assist with additional process fine-tuning.

Over time, GM found that having an engineer involved in the PICOS program who is familiar with environmental management provided important benefits for leveraging additional environmental improvement from the PICOS events. By working with suppliers on environmental improvement, GM has also, among many things, been able to

- promote the use of returnable shipping containers in lieu of single-use, disposable ones;
- communicate GM's guidelines for designing for recyclability and broadly disseminating its list of restricted or reportable chemicals; and
- communicate success stories to the supplier community as examples of what can be done.

GM also announced that suppliers will be required to certify the implementation of an EMS in their operations in conformance with ISO 14001. GM is currently developing a broader supply chain initiative, with involvement from EPA and NIST, that some participants hope will become a vehicle to integrate technical assistance on advanced manufacturing techniques and environmental improvement opportunities. Two PICOS events are described below.

Steering Column Shroud PICOS Event

GM conducted a PICOS rapid improvement event with a key supplier to enhance the cost competitiveness and on-time delivery of steering column components. The GM team used value stream mapping and the "five whys" to assess the existing process for steps that cause long lead times and delays. The assessment revealed that the supplier shipped the steering column shrouds (or casings) to an outside vendor for painting prior to final assembly with the steering column, adding significant flow time to the production process.

Using the "five whys" technique, the team asked why the shrouds needed to be painted in the first place. The answer was "because the die (plastic mold) creates flaws that need to be covered." This led the team to a simpler, less wasteful solution — improve the quality of the die, and mold the part using resin of the desired color.

After some research, and capital investment of $400,000, the supplier incorporated an injection molding process for the shrouds into the assembly line, eliminating the need for the time-consuming painting step. This project saved the supplier approximately $700,000 per year, while shortening lead times and improving on-time delivery to GM.

This lean project produced environmental benefits, although they were not needed to make the business case for pursuing the project. Elimination of the painting process step:

- eliminated seven tons per year of VOC emissions from the painting process step,
- all hazardous wastes associated with the painting process step (including clean-up rags, overspray sludge, off-spec and expired paints), and
- environmental impacts associated with transporting the shrouds to the painting vendor and back.

Thermoplastic Color Purging PICOS Event

While working with a supplier to reduce lead times and improve quality for the production of a thermoplastic molded component, a GM-facilitated team found additional waste elimination opportunities associated with color changeovers. At this time, the suppliers' operations were running seven days a week to meet customer demand.

The team found that each time the supplier changed resin colors to produce a new batch of parts, as many as 5 to 10 large plastic parts needed to be scrapped. The accumulated scrap typically would fill a 30 yard dumpster every day, resulting in $3,000 to $4,000 per week in disposal costs. In addition, the supplier consumed more resin than necessary, contributing to higher material costs.

By focusing the rapid improvement event on streamlining the die set up and color changeover process, the team was able to reduce the need to run overtime shifts to meet customer demand while eliminating a significant waste stream, as well as the extra resin and processing associated with the scrap.

Questions

Are you using reusable containers?

Are you cleaning more often than necessary?

Do any of your processes contain steps that could be eliminated by improving earlier steps?

Do your changeovers produce too much scrap?

Index